ARGUING WITH GOD

The Angry Prayers of Job

ARGUING WITH GOD

GOD

The Angry Prayers of Job

by Dale Patrick

The Bethany Press
St. Louis, Missouri

Library of Congress Cataloguing in Publication Data

Patrick, Dale.
    Arguing with God.
    Includes a paraphrastic translation of the book of Job.
    Bibliography: p.
    Includes index.
    1. Bible. O. T. Job—Criticism, interpretation, etc. 2. Bible. O. T. Job—Paraphrases, English. I. Title.
BS1415.2.P37   223'.1'06   77-818

ISBN 0-8272-0013-7

Manufactured in the United States of America

Dedicated to

    my parents,
        my wife, Mary,
           and my son, Jeremy

cover and art by Robert Naujoks

A biographical sketch:
   Dale Patrick is the fifth generation of his family to belong to the Christian Church (Disciples of Christ). He attended Oregon State College, Lewis and Clark College (BS 1960), Union Theological Seminary, N.Y., Drew University School of Theology (BD 1963), and the Graduate Theological Union (Th D 1971), Berkeley, California. He has taught Old Testament and religious thought at the Disciple-related Missouri School of Religion since 1968. An ordained minister, he lives in Columbia, Missouri, with his wife and son and a Dachshund named Perk. He has been active in the Society of Biblical Literature and the American Academy of Religion and published articles in *Christianity and Crisis, Encounter, the Journal of Biblical Literature* and *Vetus Testamentum.* This is his first book.

Contents

How This Book Came to Be

I have always had a secret desire to write poetry, but I seldom find time and inspiration. My rational mind tells me to devote myself to my biblical scholarship and theology and leave poetry to professional poets. But biblical scholars are allowed to practice whatever poetic gifts they have when they translate the poetry of the Bible. So for my personal pleasure I combine my career and love of poetry in translating biblical poetry.

I spent several months translating Job during one of my years as a doctoral candidate. I had a spring free between examinations, so I audited a course on the Book of Job taught by David Noel Freedman. I devoted my study time to translating the book and reading scholars. My old desire to be a poet mastered me. I did not just translate the book in the sober, careful way we are taught, I tried to produce a genuinely beautiful English poetic drama.

These poetic efforts were purely for my own enjoyment. I did not show them to anyone, not even my wife. What would she think of her husband spending his time writing poetry while she was earning the income to put him through school? So the manuscript was filed away when I began studying for comprehensive exams and forgotten. It remained untouched for a half dozen years.

In the meantime I struggled through my exams and dissertation and found a job teaching Old Testament to college and seminary students. After several years of teaching, I remembered that I had once translated Job and rummaged about in my files until I found the manuscript. I was pleasantly surprised by its quality so I had it mimeographed for use in classes.

The Drama of Job

Recognizing the power of Job as a drama, I began devising ways to have it performed in my classes. To recruit actors I would offer the students the option of participating in the dramatization of Job in lieu of a paper or project. This arrangement has worked out well. The students have the fun of putting on a production and developing a sense of camaraderie while contributing significantly to the class and their own knowledge of the Bible.

These dramatizations are not full performances, but dramatic readings. The actors do not memorize the lines, but simply read their parts. They do not move or gesture much. There are no costumes, no scenery, and a minimum of props. Hence, it is easy to dramatize Job, yet it is quite effective.

I have also found other opportunities to deliver my translation of Job. At various churches in mid-Missouri I have read from the translation and offered my interpretation of what's being said. I simply follow the course of the drama, reading highlights and filling in the story. Just reading with the proper passion and emphasis communicates a lot, and reflection seems to rise up right out of the drama.

After receiving consistently positive responses from students and laypeople, both to my translation and interpretation, the idea hit me to put together a book. I sent the text and some sketches of possible interpretive chapters to the editor of Bethany Press, Sherman Hanson, and he encouraged me to proceed. What interested him most about the project was my stress on the importance of prayer in the drama. Laypeople—the audience for whom the book is written—want help with prayer, but they seldom are told anything about the way the people of the Bible prayed. This book might help fill in this gap.

Job and Prayer

Yes, Job is a book about prayer. Really, it is a story of a man of prayer. He is also an angry man, one who has suffered the outrages of fortune and refuses to take it submissively. He confronts God with angry words. His words may shock you at first; you may not recognize that he is praying. What you will learn from the book is why you should recognize this as genuine, appropriate prayer.

The translation of the book comes first, the interpretive chapters follow. This order is necessary because the most important interpretive chapter is presented as a reflection of Job on his experience. One cannot reflect on an experience until he has gone through it. The other chapters belong after the reflection.

Before You Read the Translation

But before you begin reading the story of Job there are some things you need to know about the book of Job and about the way I translated and arranged it. I will also take the opportunity to present some suggestions for presenting it as a dramatic reading.

Job was remembered by the people of Israel as a righteous man who lived in the distant past and in a foreign country. No one was quite sure when he lived (no date is given) or where Uz was. As far as the Israelites were concerned, Job simply lived long ago and far away. His story is told in chapters 1 and 2 and 42:7-17 of the Book of Job. Ezekiel also mentions him, along with Noah and a man named Daniel, as an ancient righteous man (Ezek. 14:14, 20).

The story of Job told in chapters 1 and 2 and 42:7-17 is to be distinguished from the drama presented in poetic form in chapters 3:1—42:6. The prose story of Job was used by the poet of these chapters as a launching pad for a drama. He creates an entirely new character, raises new and different issues, and provides a different conclusion. The poetic drama is, as it were, a play within a story. It must be read on its own terms. The reader naturally tries to fit the two together, but this obscures the poetic drama. I actually recommend to my students that they begin with chapter 3 and return to chapters 1 and 2 after completing the book.

The story of the first two chapters—the Lord testing Job at the instigation of the Satan, Job submitting piously to the trial—does not continue into the drama. All one has to do is compare the submissive Job of chapters 1—2 to the defiant Job of chapters 3—31 and the suggestion that God tests the righteous (chapters 1—2) to Job's mocking of this idea in 10:4-7 to recognize that each must be read separately.

Why are they together? I said above that the poet used the old story as a launching pad. The story created the situation—a righteous man who suffers undeservedly—which the poet wanted to begin with. By removing the scene from the present, he could explore it in depth without threatening his audience. Moreover, the audience would have to believe in Job's righteousness.

It should be noted, by the way, that neither the original story nor the poet were worried about the anachronism of foreigners of the distant past worshiping the One God of Israel. Job and his companions were not Jews; so they would, in fact, have been polytheists. Our biblical author puts Jewish monotheistic language in their mouths. Scholars tend to date the poetic portions of the Book of Job about 500-400 B.C.

The date 500-400 B.C. is simply a scholarly guess as to when the poetic portions of the Book of Job were written. This guess is based upon the words and style of the Hebrew and the thoughts of the characters. If you want to study this subject, consult the introductions to the Bible or scholarly commentaries on the Book of Job (see Bibliography in the back of the book).

The Poetic Drama of Job

The poetic drama of Job has excited the imagination of modern readers. In earlier, more religious ages, the Job of the first two chapters was attractive as a model for living, but the Job of the dramatic poem was incomprehensible. Nowadays the reverse is true. The submissive Job is felt to be alien, but the Job who protests in Promethean spirit, who rejects the dogmas of his friends, who confronts God with the problem of evil and injustice, is felt to be a kindred soul. Believers and non-believers alike can respond to the defiant Job. For this reason, the interpretive chapters will concentrate on the poetic drama.

Something needs to be said about the description of Job 3:1—42:6 as "poetic drama." These chapters are composed as a drama. The story consists entirely of speeches given by characters. It is an unusual drama because the speeches are long and stylized, and there is no physical action. The drama is, thus, very static according to our standards. Dramatic movement occurs entirely within speeches. This makes it somewhat hard for an audience to appreciate. I suspect that it was not composed to be presented on stage but to be read. The technical term for this type of literature is "closet drama." Nevertheless, it is a drama, not a series of speeches to be contemplated in isolation from each other. The religious questions are raised and resolved in the course of the passionate interaction of characters.

Job's three friends are not individual characters but the collective voice of the religious community. There is little discernible difference between them. Their speeches are repetitive and long-winded. Their tone does change as the drama progresses; they become harsher and harsher until Job is openly condemned.

12

Job's speeches are just the opposite of his friends'. They are extremely passionate, filled with flashes of insight and unheard-of thoughts, changing from speech to speech in a definite, steady movement. If there is any problem with his speeches, it is the problem of sustaining the high-pitched passion. The reader must be sensitive to his constant changes of mood, the nuances of his ideas, the way he responds to what he has just said.

The Lord God enters the drama at the conclusion. His two-part revelation (chapters 38—39, 40—41) is couched as a cross-examination, an interrogation of Job. His own thought and feeling is concealed behind His questions. The challenge of presenting Him dramatically is to preserve His mystery, grandeur and dignity. In staging Job we have found it effective to have the performer speak through a loudspeaker to establish distance.

The Re-arrangement of the Text

It is to be noted that I have re-arranged the text and cut out some portions. What I have done and the reasons for it are presented in the Appendix. The text suffered during the years before it was included in the Bible from additions by outraged readers and by accidental displacements. The book now is something like a stained-glass window in a medieval cathedral which has been taken out and put back several times, in the process of which some pieces have gotten out of position. The book demands reconstruction by scholars to look like the original. I have in this translation reassembled it for you. My purpose is to present you with a clear, consistent and dramatically powerful text.

Much of the power of the book is in its poetry. My original motivation for translating it was to render it in beautiful English poetry. I hope that I have achieved that. No one knows why we find pleasure in the sounds and rhythms of speech or in the imaginative rendering of thoughts in images and metaphors, but we do. Like music, it delights some portion of our mind and heart that escapes the pale cast of thought. Poetry makes a simple and even commonplace idea profound and moving. It reaches to capture passions and feelings so the audience or reader can enter into the inner life of another character. The poet strives to create language equal to the occasion and to the emotions felt on the occasion.

The flow of the poetry in my translation imitates modern rhythms of speech and idiom. Most translations of Job tend to be a bit too formal and stilted for our ears. I contracted words, threw in expletives, changed finite sentences into clauses, and so forth, to free the language. I shied away from unnatural order and stodgy punctuation.

I have sought to make the language dramatic and passionate. I consistently referred statements as directly as possible to the drama itself. The Hebrew original often could be interpreted as saying something quite general, but I would seek to discover what the person was saying about his own situation. If you compare my translations with others, you will discover how I channeled the language toward its dramatic import and away from its abstract intellectual content.

A "Paraphrastic" Translation

To avoid the scorn of my Old Testament colleagues I call my translation "paraphrastic." I sought to render the sense of the poetic line, but I did not restrict myself to substituting English words for the corresponding Hebrew. What I would do is to decide what the author was saying, then compose a line fitting my poetic and dramatic requirements. In most cases, my English line resembles the Hebrew closely, but occasionally it deviates rather shockingly from a straight-forward translation.

To illustrate the way I went about translating, let's examine Job 42:5. The Hebrew of this sentence offers no difficulties. The Revised Standard Version translates it accurately:

I had heard of thee by the hearing of the ear,
but now my eye sees thee;

My translation of this same verse runs:

I had heard of You by the word of others,
but now I have encountered You in person.

I must admit that the RSV translation is more poetic, but it is nonetheless archaic. We do not use *thee* and *thou* in contemporary English. The phrase *the hearing of the ear* is rather stilted and requires explanation for the average reader. It means, as my translation puts it, that Job had prior to the revelation from the whirlwind known God through tradition communicated by teachers and fellow believers. The second line is literally false; Job has not "seen" God. What the statement means is that Job's knowledge of God is no longer mediated through others, it is the fruit of a person-to-person encounter. In both lines, I have dropped the images but retained the idea. Note too my change in punctuation.

Job As a Dramatic Reading

Finally, let me make some further suggestions for presenting Job as a dramatic reading. Job makes a powerful, beautiful, and thought-provoking presentation for the schoolroom and the church. It can be staged as a reading with relatively little effort and no expense. The readers do not have to memorize the lines, it is quite effective as a reading if the participants can read fluently and dramatically. It takes six readers—Job, his three companions Eliphaz, Bildad, and Zophar, a narrator and God. Women can play the parts as well as men.

As to staging, the performers can use their imagination. Costumes are unnecessary and probably undesirable unless one is performing Job as a stage play. In class, students wear their regular clothes. As to props we have usually had a stepladder for the person playing God to sit on and a

14

loudspeaker to amplify and distance his or her voice. The narrator may speak from a rostrum or from center stage (say, from a big black book reminding the audience of a Bible). The three companions of Job might be ranged around him, somewhat elevated so that they can "talk down" to him. When their speeches are over, they might turn their backs on him.

It is often felt that cuts are necessary for reading. Performing the full text takes about an hour and a quarter, and one doesn't usually have that much time. Moreover, some of the speeches are repetitious and dull; they were meant to be, but groups may not want to bore their audience. In case you feel it is desirable to cut the text for reading, let me suggest the portions of each speech that can be cut without distorting the drama unduly:

Job	3:7-9, 12, 23-24
Eliphaz	4:10-11, 5:3-5, 14, 21-22
Job	6:5-7, 18-20, 23, 7:10, 15-16
Bildad	8:14-17, 22, 26:6, 9
Job	9:8-9, 13, 18, 25-31, 10:10, 17
Zophar	11:9, 27:18-19, 22, 11:16-18, 20
Job	12:8, 15, 19, 22, 25, 13:2, 11, 18-19, 14:6b, 11
Eliphaz	15:5, 8, 13, 23, 26-33
Job	16:9-14, 17:7-9, 14
Bildad	18:8-11, 15-16, 18-19, 21
Job	19:8-12, 15, 18-19
Zophar	20:12-19, 24-26, 28-29
Job	21:12, 24:4, 23, 21:20-21, 24, 32-33
Eliphaz	22:8, 11, 17, 20, 28
Job	23:11
Narrator	27:12, 28:4, 6, 11, 14, 16, 18-19, 26
God	38:9, 14-15, 34-38, 39:7-8, 21-25, 28-29, 40:13, 31
Narrator	42:11-17

Good luck and on with the show!

Translation

Narrator

1:1 There once lived a man Job, in the region of Uz, a blameless and
2 upright man who revered God and did not injure his neighbor. He
3 had seven sons and three daughters. His property consisted of
seven thousand sheep and goats, three thousand camels, five
hundred yoke of oxen, five hundred asses, and a large corps of
servants. So he was one of the wealthiest men in all the east.

4   His sons gathered and held banquets on each one's birthday, and they would invite their three sisters to eat and drink with
5   them. When the days of the feast had run their course, Job would bless them and rise early in the morning to sacrifice for his children, one sacrifice for each, for Job thought to himself, "Perhaps my sons have sinned and cursed God in their hearts." Job followed this same procedure year by year.

6   Now the day came when the sons of God appeared before the
7   Lord, and the Devil's Advocate was among them. And the Lord said to the Devil's Advocate: "From where have you come?" And the Devil's Advocate replied: "O, from roving about in the world and walking here and there in it."

8   And the Lord said to the Devil's Advocate: "What do you think of my servant Job? There is no one like him on earth, a blameless and
9   upright man who reveres God and does not injure his neighbor." And
10 the Devil's Advocate replied to the Lord: "Does Job revere God for nothing? Haven't You put a protective fence around him, his house
11 and property? You have blessed his every enterprise and his possessions overflow. But if You were to deal him and everything he
12 owns a great blow, would he not curse You to Your face?" And the Lord said to the Devil's Advocate: "I put everything that belongs to him at your disposal. Only do not touch the man himself." So the Devil's Advocate left the Lord's presence.

13   And the day came when Job's sons and daughters ate and drank
14 wine at the house of their elder brother. And a messenger came running to Job and said: "The oxen were plowing and the asses were
15 grazing beside them, when some Arabs fell on us and rustled the
16 animals and killed the servants. I alone escaped to tell you." Before he could finish speaking, another came and said: "Lightning descended from the sky and destroyed the sheep and their shepherds.
17 I alone escaped to tell you." Before he could finish speaking yet another came and said: "The Chaldeans formed into three columns and made a raid upon the camels and took them away after killing
18 their tenders with swords, and I alone escaped to bring the news." Before he could finish speaking yet another messenger came and said:
19 "Your sons and daughters were eating and drinking wine in the house of their elder brother and a great wind swept in from the desert and struck the house from all sides, and it fell upon them and all are dead. I alone escaped to tell you."

20   Job got up and ripped off his clothes and shaved his head and fell
21 to the earth and prayed: "Naked I came from my mother's womb, and naked shall I return to nothing. The Lord has given, the Lord
22 has taken away. Blessed be the Lord's name." And Job did not sin or blame God.

2:1   And the day came when the sons of God appeared before the Lord,
2   and the Devil's Advocate was among them. The Lord asked the

Devil's Advocate: "From where have you come?" And the Devil's Advocate replied: "O, from roving about in the world and walking
3 here and there in it." And the Lord said to the Devil's Advocate: "Well, what do you think of my servant Job? There is no one like him on earth, a blameless and upright man who reveres God and does not injure his neighbor. Even now he holds tight to his integrity
4 after you have incited Me to attack him without due cause." But the Devil's Advocate replied to the Lord: "Skin for skin! So what're
5 his possessions to him? But his life is most precious to him. If You
6 were to strike his bone and his flesh, would he not curse You to Your
7 face?" And the Lord said to the Devil's Advocate: "He is at your disposal. Only do not take his life." And the Devil's Advocate left the Lord's presence and struck Job with festering sores from the soles
8 of his feet to the top of his head. And Job scratched himself with
9 potsherds and sat in an ashheap. And his wife said to him: "So you
10 still cling to your integrity? Why don't you curse God and die?" But Job replied to her: "You are talking foolishness. We gladly accepted what God gave us when it was good. Should we now refuse to accept the bad?" And Job did not sin throughout by what he said.
11   Now three friends of Job heard the news of his misfortunes and each man came from his home, Eliphaz from Teman, Bildad from

Shuh, and Zophar from Naamath. They arranged to go together to
12 console and to comfort him. While they were yet at a distance they
saw him but could not recognize him, and they raised up their voices
13 and wept and ripped off their clothes and flung ashes on their
heads. They sat with him on the ground seven days and seven
nights, and no one spoke a word to him, for they saw how great his
sorrow was.

3:1   Then Job opened his mouth and cursed the day of his birth.

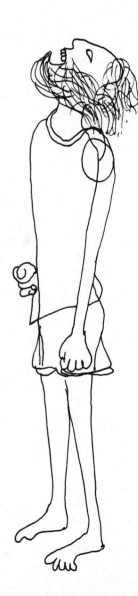

3:2   **Job**

3 Damn the day of my birth!
   The night when they shouted "A boy!"
4 I would have that day be dark,
   and God not seek it out
   nor light shine upon it.
5 Let black and deep shadows claim it,
   a cloud hover over it,
   an eclipse grip it with fear.
6 I would have that night removed,
   not combined with the days of the year
   or entered in the calendar of months.

7 Let that night be barren
without a joyful shout to break its silence.
8 Perhaps spell-binders and wierd magicians
can curse my day of birth
9 so its twilight stars will not come out
and dawn will not appear on time
and day not break through the dark.
10 For it did not stop the womb's opening for me
nor hide my eyes from suffering.

11 Why didn't I die within the womb
and come forth stillborn?
12 Why did knees cradle me?
Why were there breasts for me to suck on?
13 Dead would I now lie and quiet
and asleep, resting among
14 the kings and statesmen of the world
who built ruins for themselves,
15 princes who hoarded gold,
whose houses bulged with silver.

16 Why was I not a buried miscarriage,
a fetus which did not see light?
17 In Sheol the restive desist from agitating
and the exhausted finally get a rest.
18 Its prisoners live quietly together.
They hear no warden command.
19 Both small and great are there
and a slave is free from his master.

20 Why does He give light to the sufferer,
life to the bitter in heart,
21 who long for death but do not find it,
and search for it rather than hidden treasure,
22 who would leap in exultation to feel the tomb,
dance gaily to find the grave?
23 —To a man whose way is hidden from him,
whom God barricades in?
24 Look at me: For my meals I'm served moans,
and groans are poured me to drink.
25 My worst fears have materialized
and whatever I dreaded finds me out.
26 I cannot relax nor be quiet
nor rest, for suffering comes and comes.

Eliphaz the Temanite

2 Will you grow impatient if one ventures a word with you?
  But who can keep back the words?
3 And once you set others straight
  and steadied the hands of the weak.
4 Your words kept the falling afoot
  and you stiffened wobbly knees.
5 But now when something happens to you, you chafe.
  When misfortune strikes you too, you collapse.
6 Aren't you confident in your piety?
  Can't you base your hope on your exemplary life?
7 Now just think back! Who ever perished who was innocent?
  Where were honest men swept away?

8 Again and again I have seen those who cultivate injustice
 and sow trouble harvest it.
9 God's breath scorches them like a hot, tropical wind,
 by the gust of His wrath they are consumed.
10 The lion roars and the panther screams,
 but the fangs of the young lion break,
11 the leopard dies for lack of prey,
 and the lion-whelps scatter.

12 Once I experienced a secret revelation.
 My ear heard a whisper
13 and my eye saw phantoms of the night
 when complete sleep falls upon men.
14 Terror seized me and trembling
 until my frame quivered.
15 A spirit glided by my face
 and my hair stood up on my skin.
16 It stood still but I could not make out its shape
 though a form was before my eyes.
 And I heard a voice in the still air:
17 "Can mere man be righteous before God?
 A man be blameless before his Maker?
18 Not even in His servants does He trust
 and He finds fault in His angels.
19 How much more the creatures of mud houses
 with dirt foundations,
20 who are crushed from morning till nightfall,
 destroyed year on year without notice?
21 Isn't their vaunted dignity torn from them?
 They die, yes, and still in ignorance."

5:1 Why don't you pray? But who would answer you?
 To which divine being would you turn?
2 Give heed: Bitterness kills the fool,
 and anger slays the impudent.
3 I myself have watched the fool strike root,
 but suddenly his dwelling rots,
4 and his sons discover safety to be a receding mirage.
 They get defrauded in the gate of the law
 and no one comes to their defense.
5 The hungry rob his cropland for food
 and it is taken over by thorns and thistles.
6 For despair does not simply spring up from the dust
 nor does trouble just sprout from the soil.
7 Rather, a man gives birth to his own misery,
 just as sparks from a fire fly upward.

8 If I were you, I would seek God
 and set my case before the Lord,

9 who does great and mysterious things,
  marvels and wonders without number,
10 who provides rain for the surface of the ground
  and allots water for each field,
11 who raises those who are down to positions of honor,
  and those in despair ascend to salvation,
12 who frustrates the designs of crafty men
  so their labors cannot manufacture salvation,
13 who defeats the wise at their own craft
  and aborts the plans of twisted minds.
14 During the day they encounter darkness
  and grope about at noon as if it were night.
15 But He rescues the helpless from the swordblade
  and the poor from the clutch of the powerful.
16 There is hope for the powerless
  and injustice shuts its mouth.
17 So happy is the man whom God punishes.
  Do not refuse His disciplining,
18 for He wounds only in order to bind up,
  He injures that His hands might heal.
19 He will bring you through six disasters,
  yea, through seven you'll go unscathed.
20 In famine He will stave off your death
  and rescue you from the sword in wartime.
21 You will be enarmored against tongue-lashing
  and when violence threatens, you will not shudder.
22 You will laugh at carnage and starvation
  and will not even fear wild beasts.
23 You will be in league with field-stones
  and at harmony with the beasts of the wild.
24 You will know that your home is safe,
  and inspect your homestead and miss nothing.
25 And you will know that your offspring abound,
  that you have as many descendants
  as there are grassblades on the ground.
26 You will go down into the grave after a long, productive life
  like grain harvested at threshing time.
27 Now consider what we have examined: Isn't it so?
  Give it a hearing and adopt it.

2 If only the full weight of my suffering were measured
and my numerous causes for anger laid on the scales,
3 they would outweigh the sand of the seashore.
That's why my words are savage.
4 Yes indeed, my blood sucks in the poison arrows
flung by a God of war,
and He readies His torture-chambers for me.
5 Does an ass bray over fresh grass?
Does an ox low over good forage?
6 Can tasteless food be eaten without salt?
Does egg-white have any flavor?
7 My mouth refuses to touch this fare,
it makes me sick.

8 How I wish that my request would be answered,
that God would give me what I crave,
9 that He would go ahead and crush me completely,
that He would let go His hand and finish it.
10 That would be some comfort to me:
I would find joy in its finality.
For I have not disobeyed the Holy One
and put an end to myself.

11 What urge have I to endure?
To what end do I prolong my life?
12 Is my stamina the substance of stones?
Is my flesh bronze?
13 No, I am helpless.
Support escapes me.

14 A fainting man deserves the loyalty of friends
even if he has turned sour on religion.
15 But my brothers betray me like an intermittent stream,
like a creek which overflows its banks,
16 muddy from ice,
swollen from melting snow,
17 but which vanishes during the hot season,
dries up under the burning sun.
18 Caravans venture from the road,
go into the wild and perish.
19 Say, a caravan from Tema is searching for water
or traders from Sheba place great hope in a wadi.
20 Their expectancy leads to utter disappointment,
they come to the streambed and find dry-dirt.

21 Such you've become to me!
You see my fate and shrink back.
22 Have I said, Give me presents?
Offer a bribe for me from your wealth?
23 Get me released from the constraint of a lawsuit?
Ransom me from the clutch of overlords?
24 Teach me, and I'll drop my complaint,
explain to me where I have gone wrong.
25 What harm do honest words do?
Why do they deserve your censure?
26 Do you attempt to censure words,
the senseless syllables of a desperate man?
27 You cast lots over an innocent,
barter over your friend.
28 But now please look me in the face!
Would I lie to your faces?
29 Stop before you do a great wrong.
Back off, my right is at stake.
30 Has my tongue made a false accusation?
Doesn't my mouth know when it lies?

7:1 Isn't a man's life on earth a duty,
his days the hard labor of a workman,
2 like a sweaty slave who lives for evening shade,
a hired man who works in anticipation of his wages?
3 So I'm paid with empty months,
and my nights reward me with tedium.
4 When I lie down I wish it were morning,
for I toss to and fro without sleep from dusk to dawn.
5 Worms cover my flesh,
my scabs dry, my skin hardens, cracks and runs.

6 My days move more quickly than a weaver's shuttle
to reach my future's end.
7 Remember, Lord, my life is but a breath.
Never again will my eye see beauty.
8 The eye which sees me will never behold me again.
While Your eye is on me I will vanish forever.
9 As a cloud fades and dissipates,
so one who enters the underworld does not come out.
10 He does not return to his house again,
his home no longer recalls him.

11 But I will not check my mouth!
I will proclaim the agony of my spirit
and open up my bitter soul.
12 Am I the Sea, am I Tannin the sea-monster,
that You should put me under guard?
13 When I think, "My bed will give me comfort,
my couch will ease my sore mind,"

14 You terrify me with bad dreams
and descend on me with visions.
15 I would choose to strangle myself
but I loathe death more than suffering.
16 I will not live forever.
Leave me in peace for I have but a few days left.

17 What is man that You take him so seriously
and even set Your heart upon him,
18 and visit him every morning,
examine him every moment?
19 Will You never look away from me?
Won't You even desist while I swallow my spit?
20 So I sin—How does it concern You, O Spy of mankind?
Why do You set me up as an object of attack?
How do I burden You?
21 Why not put up with my sin
and ignore my guilt?
But now I am about to lie down in the dirt.
When You desire to see me, I will be no more.

8:1 **Bildad the Shuhite**

2 How long will you spew forth such things?
Your tirade is pure wind.
3 Does God pervert justice?
Does Almighty God pervert the right?
4 Your sons sinned against Him
and He condemned them to the consequences.
5 But if you look to God
and pray for His mercy,
6 if you are indeed clear and straight,
He will awaken to you
and restore you to your rightful place.

7 Though your beginning may be small,
your future will rise to greatness.

8 Make an inquiry into past generations
and study what our fathers found to be true,
9 for we were born but yesterday and know nothing,
our days on earth are a mere shadow.
10 Can they not teach you and tell you something?
Profound words have proceeded from their intellects:
11 "Does papyrus grow well outside the swamps?
Can the reed grow in dry places?
12 After it has just sprouted
it yellows before any other plant, without even being cut."
13 So it is with the life of everyone who forgets God.
He has no future at all.
14 His source of confidence is a thin thread
no stronger than a spider web.
15 When he leans on his house it falls,
when he takes hold of it it buckles.
16 He may thrive in the sunlight
and his shoots spread out over the garden,
17 but then his roots twine around a rockpile
or hit bedrock.
18 When he is removed from his spot,
it disowns him, saying, "I've never seen you."
19 This is the kind of joy he receives for his life,
and another sprouts up in his soil.

20 Thus God will never reject an innocent man
nor support an evil-doer.
21 Once again He will fill your mouth with laughter
and your lips with "hurrah!"
22 Your enemies will be covered with shame
and the wicked will lose their homes.

25:2 To God belong dominion and fearful majesty.
He it is who creates the harmonious order from His heights.
3 Can His servants be counted or numbered?
Who is hidden from His splendor?
26:5 The shades tremble beneath,
the primeval ocean and its inhabitants.
6 The underworld is naked before Him,
the netherworld has no curtain.
7 He suspends the northern pillars over the void
and plants the earth in mid-air,
8 dams water in dense clouds
to hold back the flood,
9 hides the face of the moon
and spreads out clouds over it.

10 He pounded out the vault of heaven over the primeval waters
    as a boundary of light and dark.
11 The sky-pillars sway back and forth,
    trembling at His rebuke.
12 He has calmed the sea by force
    and defeated Rahab the dragon by cunning.
13 By His wind He bottled the sea
    and His hand pierced the fleeing sky-serpent.
14 Lo, these are but hints of His vast activity.
    We get only an inkling of what He does.
    Who can imagine the full thunder of His power?

25:4 How then can a man be righteous before God?
    A mere mortal, born of woman, be clean?
  5 Even the moon does not shine brightly
    nor are the stars spotless in His eyes.
  6 How much less man, a worm,
    one of the human race, a maggot!

26:1   **Job**

  2 My how you've rushed to the aid of the all-powerless One
    and strengthened His feeble arm!
  3 Since He doesn't know enough you have decided to advise Him
    and reveal the workings of the mind.
  4 With whom do you exchange these wise words?
    Who inspired you?
 9:2 But yes, what you say is all too true:
    How can a man establish his righteousness before God?
  3 If he decides to bring Him to trial,
    he could not make one of a thousand charges stand.

  4 His mind is so wise, His spirit so forceful—
    who has ever challenged Him and survived?
  5 He crumbles mountains without second thought,
    He overturns them in His wrath,
  6 shakes the earth at its foundations
    until its supports stagger,
  7 orders the sun not to shine
    and seals off the stars.
  8 Has He not laid out these vast heavens by Himself
    and subdued the boiling seas of chaos,
  9 made the Great Bear, Orion and Pleiades
    and the constellations of the southern sky?

10 How terrible and mysterious are His deeds!
  How infinite His wonders are marvels!
11 And lo, He passes by but I do not perceive Him,
  glides by without a glimpse.
12 When He decides to rob and kidnap who can dissuade Him?
  Can cry out to Him, "What are You doing?"
13 A god could not turn back his anger.
  Even Rahab's demons would knuckle under.

14 Do I really want to argue with Him?
  How would I choose my words?
15 Though I am in the right I could not refute Him.
  I would have to implore mercy from the one I accuse.
16 If I summoned Him to court and He responded,
  I could not be sure that He would listen to my voice.
17 He would smash me with a howling wind,
  increase my wounds without justification.
18 He would not allow me to gain my breath,
  but fill me with bitterness.
19 Is it a trial of strength? He is strongest.
  Is it a matter of law? Who can arraign Him?
20 Were I to prove my innocence He would condemn me.
  Were I to prove my integrity He would declare me guilty.
21 I plead innocent!
  I accept the risk!
  I despise my life!
22 What difference does it make?
  He murders the innocent and guilty alike.
23 When a disaster suddenly strikes,
  He laughs at the trials of the innocent.
24 The earth has been delivered over to the forces of evil
  and He turns the eyes of justice the other way.
  If not He, who?

25 My days lunge forward faster than a runner,
  escape without a glimpse of happiness.
26 They glide along like reed-skiffs,
  like an eagle swooping upon its victim.

27 If I say, I will forget my grievance,
  I will relax my face and smile,
28 I tense up anticipating the next blow,
  well knowing that You will not acquit me.
29 I am to be condemned:
  Why then do I struggle so in vain?
30 If I washed myself as clean as snow,
  if I scrubbed my hands with lye,
31 You would rub me in the dirt
  until my own clothes would despise me.

32 If only He were a man, an equal,
   that I might bring Him to task,
   that we might join legal arguments.
33 If only there were an arbiter with power
   to decide the dispute between us.
34 Let Him but lift His rod
   and stop overwhelming me with fear,
35 and I would speak out fearlessly,
   for I am not anxious about myself.

10:1 I hold my existence in contempt!
   Let me issue my complaint against it,
   speak openly out of my rancid soul.
2 I will say to God: "Do not condemn me!
   Give me the legal grounds of Your verdict!"
3 Do You find pleasure in tormenting
   and discarding the work of Your own hands?
4 Do You have physical eyes like a man
   and peer out through them to see?
5 Do Your days have morning and evening?
   Is Your life-span about the same as ours?
6 Then why do You search for some guilt in me
   and seek to discover my sinfulness by experiment?
7 You know that I am not guilty
   but there is no release from Your grip.

8 Your own hand formed and shaped me,
   and now You turn around and destroy me.
9 Remember, Lord, how You made me of clay.
   Will You now grind me to dust?
10 Have You not produced me like milk
   and hardened me like cheese?
11 You clothed me in skin and flesh,
   weaved me together with bones and sinews.
12 You were loyal and loving
   and my breathing was kept in Your care.
13 But You have hidden these things from Your heart.
   I know You planned this from the beginning.

14 If I sin You are watching
   and will not release me from my guilt.
15 If I do wrong, woe!
   But if I do right I cannot lift up my head.
   I am disgraced and humiliated.
16 If I do raise it You stalk me like a lion
   and work wonders against me,
17 call up Your witnesses against me,
   flood me with sorrows,
   and order up fresh torments for me!

18 Why did You deliver me from the womb?
   Why wasn't I stillborn before an eye had seen me?
19 Then would I be as though I had never been,
   carried from the womb to the grave.
20 My days are few, let me be.
   Leave me in peace that I might flash a brief smile.
21 Straightway I will go and not return,
   to a land of dark and shadow,
22 a night land, gloom, dead-black,
   black shining in black.

11:1   **Zophar the Naamathite**

11:2 Shall such verbosity go unanswered?
     Shall he win his case by smooth oratory?
   3 Shall your glib speech silence men?
     Shall you blaspheme and no one censure?
   4 You say, "My doctrine is pure."
     You may be clear in your own eyes,
   5 but if God would just speak,
     and open His lips to you
   6 and explain the secrets of wisdom
     and multiplex nature of understanding!
     Be it known that God exacts less of you
     than you deserve.

   7 Can you explore the divine abyss
     or discover an outer limit to Almighty God?

31

8 How will you attain the heights of heaven?
   How will you learn what is deeper than Sheol?
9 Doesn't He stretch beyond the ends of the land,
   beyond the breadth of the sea?
10 If He passes by and imprisons
   and condemns, who can restrain Him?
11 For He knows human failing.
   When He observes evil,
   won't He make note of it?

27:13 Let's review the lot of a rebel against God,
      what inheritance a violent man receives from Him:
  14 If he fathers many sons it is for war-victims,
     Or they lack enough bread.
  15 Those who survive him are buried during a plague.
     His widow does not mourn.
  16 Though he amass silver as dust heaps up
     and assemble a massive wardrobe,
  17 he assembles clothes for the righteous to wear,
     and the pure in heart will divide his silver.
  18 The house he builds is like that of a spider
     or like the hut a sentry makes—
  19 he lies down in splendor,
     but he opens his eyes to see it gone.
  20 Panic descends upon him during the day
     and a hurricane carries him away during the night.
  21 An east wind hoists him up and leaves;
     it sweeps him away from his soil.
  22 It descends upon him without pity
     and he flees headlong from its pursuit.
  23 Men will clap their hands at him in derision
     and hiss at him for his fate.

27:8 What hope is there for an irreverent man?
     Will God not demand his soul?
   9 Will God listen to his scream
     when disaster descends upon him?
  10 Will he ever enjoy divine favor?
     Will God meet him every time?

11:13 But if you take control of your heart
      and let your hands ascend toward God,
  14 if you remove any filth from your hand
     and do not allow vice to inhabit your household,
  15 then you will raise up your face without shame
     and be given a solid foundation.
  16 You will leave your suffering behind,
     will remember it as water over the mill.
  17 Your life will rise to its meridian;
     the gloom will break as at the dawn.

18 You will be secure in your future,
   look around and lie down in security.
19 You will repose without unrest
   and many will vie for your favor.
20 But the eyes of the wicked grow dim watching,
   for every way of escape has been cut off
   and their hopes are never fulfilled.

12:1   **Job**

2 No doubt you are learned men
   and wisdom will die with you.
3 But I have a mind as well as you.
   I'm not your inferior.
   Who doesn't know what you've said?
7 Just ask the beasts and they will teach you,
   and the birds of the sky will tell you,
8 or the reptiles of the ground will give you instruction,
   and the fish of the sea will recount it to you.
9 Which of all these creatures does not know
   that all things are the Lord's handiwork?
10 His hand holds the pulse-beat of every life,
   the breathing of all human flesh.
13 Wisdom and power are His,
   strength and insight.
14 He breaks down and no one can rebuild;
   He imprisons and no one can break out.
15 He shuts off the rain and there is drought,
   and lets it loose and water floods the earth.
16 He possesses power and providence,
   and both deceiver and deceived belong to Him.

17 He strips statesmen naked
   and throws judges into doubt,
18 lets loose judgment on kings
   and puts them in waist-chains,
19 exiles priests stripped of their office
   and subverts established orders,
20 silences the advice of the trustworthy
   and takes away the elders' power to decide,
21 pours scorn upon the nobility
   and rips off the belts of lords.
22 He exposes the depths of darkness
   and brings dark shadows to light,

23 raises nations to greatness only to undo them,
   extends a country's border and then enslaves it,
24 turns the minds of the people's leaders awry
   and leads them into a pathless waste.
25 There they grope in the invisible darkness—
   He sends them stumbling about as if drunk.

13:1 Yes indeed, my eye has seen it all;
     my ear has heard it and confirmed it.
 2 I too possess learning, indeed, as great as yours.
   I'm not at all your inferior.
 3 But I will speak to Almighty God,
   for I desire to argue my case before Him.
 4 As for the three of you:
   You whitewash with lies
   and offer empty abstractions as comfort.
 5 If only you would keep silent!
   Let silence show your wisdom!
 6 Listen for once to my defense
   and pay attention to the charges that I bring.
 7 Will you make dishonest assertions in God's behalf,
   even peddle fraud for Him?
 8 Will you unbalance the scales of justice in His favor?
   Do you plead God's case for Him?
 9 How good would it go if He examined you?
   Or would you deceive Him as one does a man?
10 He will arraign and condemn you
   if you continue to secretly judge unfairly.
11 Won't His majesty seize you with terror
   and panic spread over you when you stand before Him?
12 Your maxims are dusty proverbs;
   your arguments are clay.

13 Keep quiet and let me speak,
   and let come what may!
14 I will seize my flesh in my teeth
   and take my life in my own hands.
15 Though He kill me—and I expect Him to—
   yet I will argue my case before Him!
16 This itself may be my salvation,
   for the unrighteous cannot appear before Him.
17 Hear my words!
   Let them ring in your ears!
18 For now I will muster my arguments.
   I know that I am in the right.
19 Who will join arguments with me?
   —Then I would shut up and die.

20 But, Lord, I must make two requests,
   and then I will not need to hide myself from You:
21 Get Your hands off me
   and don't overpower me with Your deity!
22 Then call and I will answer,
   or I can speak and You respond to me.
23 What great evil am I guilty of?
   Expose my wrong, my sin before my eyes.
24 Why, why have You hidden Your face
   and treated me like an enemy?
25 Why do You chase a windblown leaf,
   pursue a sun-dried straw?
26 For You have inscribed bitter things upon me
   and branded me with my childhood sins.
27 You have locked my feet in stocks
   and pegged my soles to the ground
   and then watched how I ran.

14:1 Mortal man, born of woman,
   but a few days to live, and how tedious they are
   2 Like a flower, a person blooms and fades,
   like a fleeting shadow, he comes and goes.

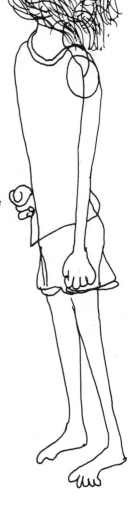

13:28 He rots like festering tissue,
     like a moth-eaten robe he decays.
14:3 And upon such a creature You fix Your gaze
     and drag him before Your bar of judgment.
  5 A man's days are bounded.
     You number his months, decree his death,
     and he cannot extend the date.
  6 Look away from him and leave him in peace!
     Let him enjoy his day like a day-laborer.

  7 Now a tree has hope:
     When it is cut down it sprouts again;
     its shoots do not die with it.
  8 When its roots age in the soil
     and its trunk above ground dies,
  9 at the scent of water it will bud
     and send up shoots like a seedling.

10 But a man dies and his corpse is still,
     a human stops breathing—and where is he?
11 Water vanishes from a lake,
     a river dwindles and dries up.
12 A man lies down and does not rise up.
     Never again does he stir under heaven
     or awaken from his sleep.

13 If only You would hide me in the underworld,
     conceal me there until Your wrath has passed,
     and appoint a time to meet me.
14 But how can a dead man still be alive?
     O that I might endure my hard days until relief comes.
15 Lord, if only You would call I would answer You,
     if only You yearned for the work of Your hands.
16 For then You would keep count of my steps,
     but not keep watching my sins.
17 My evil would be bundled in a bag—
     You would cover up my misdeeds.

18 But the crumbling mountains weathers,
     its granite rock erodes,
19 water wears away the stones
     and flash-floods wash away the topsoil.
     Likewise You destroy all human hope:
20 You assault a man time after time and he passes;
     You weather his face to leather, then send him away.
21 His sons are honored, but he does not know it,
     or they are humiliated, but he is not conscious.
22 He feels only the pain of his decaying flesh,
     and his soul mourns over itself.

15:1 **Eliphaz the Temanite**

2 Would one who is truly wise make wind his thesis
   and bluster his supporting argument?
3 What does such an argument achieve?
   What is gained by such worthless words?
4 You violate the bounds of piety
   and disturb our divine meditation,
5 for your twisted heart instructs your lips
   and you elect the forked tongue of a schemer.
6 Your own mouth convicts you, not I.
   Your lips are a witness against you.

7 Were you the first man to be born?
   Were you brought forth before the hills?
8 Have you been privy to God's thoughts?
   Do you have a monopoly on wisdom?
9 What do you know that we do not?
   Does your mind perceive some mystery that is beyond us?
10 Both age and experience are with us—
   why, our combined age is greater than your father's.

11 Are God's mercies too small for you?
   Does His word move too slow for you?

12 Why do you let your passions master your mind?
   Why do your eyes flash?

13 You see, you've turned your ire on God
   and lost control of your mouth.

14 What in human nature is worthy of purity?
   How could a creature born like an animal be righteous?

15 He does not even trust in His holy angels
   and the heavens are tainted with sin.

16 How much more a being which is profane, even foul,
   mortal man, who drinks imperfection like water!

17 Let me describe to you—now hear me out!—
   let me describe what I have learned from observation.

18 It is the teaching of wise men
   and well-known to the ancients.

20 A troublemaker writhes in pain all his days,
   and those days are definitely numbered.

21 Alarm sounds in his ears.
   In peacetime a raider invades.

22 He's afraid of the dark;
   the sword lurks for him.

23 He flees being a vulture's meal.
   He knows that the day of darkness is ready at hand.

24 Anxiety and pressure plague him;
   he's like a king always preparing for war.

25 For he has lifted his hand against God
   and entered into combat with the Almighty.

26 He charges about, shielded
27 by fat on his face
   and flab on his waist.

28 He will inhabit desolate cities,
   houses left empty,
   falling into heaps of ruins.

29 He will not gain wealth,
   and he will not plant an enduring estate.

30 He will not escape the dark.
   His sprouts will be scorched by flames,
   and his fruit will be blown off by the wind.

32 When his life is not yet finished
   he will no longer break out in spring-green leaves.

33 Rather, he will be like a grapevine stripped of its clusters,
   or an olive tree which sheds its blooms early.

34 Yes indeed, the family of an irreligious man is sterile,
   and fire destroys the household of one who buys off justice.

35 He engenders agony and fathers hardship,
   and the womb prepares a false hope.

16:1   **Job**

  2   I think I've heard this before!
       Some comforters you three are!
  3   Where is the bottom to this verbal abyss?
       Why do you feel you must refute me?
  4   I too could orate as you do
       if only our positions were reversed!
       I could compose ringing phrases over you
       and make grand gestures with my head.
  5   I could "edify" you with my mouth
       and offer "tender sympathy" with my lips.

  6   It's no use speaking; It doesn't ease the throbbing.
       But why stop? None of it would depart.
  7   Even now, when I am down, He wears me out.
       You've made my circle of friends a wasteland.
  8   And You erode away my body to witness against me!
       My leanness and hollow eyes—incriminating evidence!
  9   His anger claws and mauls me,
       He grinds His teeth at me.

12 I was going my way quietly, relaxed, unsuspecting
and He pounced,
caught me by the neck and jerked and twisted.
He set me up as a target,

13 His archers took careful aim
and struck my gut without a miss
until my entrails seep out and run to the ground.

14 He sends His battering ram to breach my defenses,
then storms me like an infantryman.

15 I have stitched sackcloth on my skin
and thrust my dignity in the dust.

16 My face burns red from weeping,
and deep shadows hang over my eye-sockets.

17 Yet I've not been proven guilty!
Even my lament is pure!

18 O earth, do not cover my blood!
Do not let my outcry find a resting place!

19 Even now I have a witness in heaven,
on high there is one who will testify.

20 I have poured out tears to God
to find a friend for me

21 who would intervene with God for a man
as a person does for his friend.

17:3 Please, Lord, deposit my pledge with You.
Who else would take the risk of vouching for me?

16:22 But now my numbered years come to a close,
and I will soon walk the path of no return.

17:1 My spirit diminishes; my days flicker.
There is my grave.

2 And mockers for my companions!
My gaze is fixed on their sneers.

4 You've made them stupid!

6 You've made me a satire before a mass audience,
and they spit in my face.

7 My eyes grow dull from sorrow,
and my body has wasted to a shadow.

11 My days pass away, my plans are dashed,
all that I wanted from life.

12 Night becomes day,
light mingles with darkness.

13 If I accept Sheol as my home
and make my bed in the darkness,

14 address the grave, "My father,"
the worms, "My mother and my sister,"

15 then where will my hope be?
Who will watch over my hope?

16 Will it descend with me into Sheol?
   Will we sink into the dust together?

18:1   **Bildad the Shuhite**

2 How long will you lay verbal traps?
  Let us have order, then we can speak!
3 Are we to be classified as cattle?
  Do you consider us dumb animals?
4 You tear your guts to pieces in rage!
  Shall the earth be abandoned for your sake?
  Its undergirding be removed from its position?

5 No, soon the light of the evildoer goes out;
  his fire-flame fails,
6 the light in his room darkens,
  the lamp over his head burns down.
7 His long stride becomes a hesitant step
  and his own schemes bring him down.
8 Yes, he is led into the trap by his own feet
  and becomes entangled in its netting.
9 Trap-jaws grab him by the heel,
  and a noose tightens about him.
10 A snare is laid for him on the ground;
   a pitfall dug upon his footpath.
11 There are hostile movements on every side,
   and he feels a pursuer at his back.
12 His power and wealth become exhausted,
   and misfortune prepares for his fall.
13 Disease eats away his skin;
   a killing ailment feeds on his limbs.
14 He is hauled away from the security of his home
   and led before the king of terrors.
15 Fire is set in his tent;
   brimstone is scattered over his home.
16 Underneath, his roots dry up,
   and above, his stem turns brown.
17 His memory vanishes from history
   and his name is forgotten in the streets.
18 His compatriots thrust him from light to darkness,
   banish him from civilization.
19 He has no offspring or descendant among his people,
   no survivor where he lived his life.

20 From east to west men witness his fate in fear,
    shudder at the lesson his end teaches.
21 In conclusion: Such are the living conditions of an evil man;
    the sanctuary of one who does not know God.

19:1   **Job**

2 How long will you torture me
    and torment me with your words?
3 At least ten times you've lectured me!
    O no, you're not ashamed to wrong me!
4 And even if my lament has broken bounds,
    my error concerns me alone.
5 Do you really intend to exalt yourselves over me
    and hold my humiliation against me?
6 Can't you see that God has subverted me
    and cast His net over me?

7 I scream "Murder!" But receive no answer.
    I cry out for help but receive no redress.
8 He blocks my path; I can't pass;
    He hides my way in darkness.
9 He strips off my honor
    and removes the crown from my head.
10 He breaks me down, I am ruined.
    He uproots my hope like a tree.
11 He has turned against me in a fit of anger,
    indeed, decided to treat me as an enemy.
12 His troops move against me en masse
    and build seigeworks at my gate
    and encamp about my home.

13 He has alienated my own brothers,
    and my acquaintances are estranged from me.
14 My intimates and close friends abandon me,
    and the servants of my own house desert me.
15 The maidservants treat me as an outsider;
    to them I am a stranger.
16 I call to my slave but he does not respond
    though I plead with him softly.
17 My presence is repulsive to my wife;
    I am disgusting to relatives.
18 Even small children despise me.
    When I rise, they jeer and taunt me.

19 All the men of my society betray me;
   the very ones whom I love turn away.
21 Have mercy on me! Mercy! You who are my friends!
   For the hand of God has struck me!
22 Why do you persecute me like God?
   Aren't you satisfied with my flesh?

23 O that my words were written down!
   O that they were inscribed on copper!
24 Engraved by iron styles on lead!
   Chiseled in stone for all time!
25 For I am certain that my vindicator exists,
   one who will someday testify on this spot.
26 After my skin has decayed away;
   without my flesh I shall see God,
27 a God who is on my side.
   I will blink my eyes,
   and He will no longer be alien and hostile.

   I feel relaxed inside.

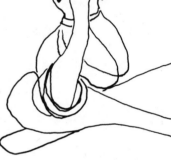

20:1   **Zophar the Naamathite**

 2 How my thoughts reverberate
    because of the turmoil inside me!
 3 I have had to listen to an insulting diatribe.
    A spirit within me keeps speaking back.

 4 Have you not learned from antiquity,
    from the time when man became established on earth,
 5 that the revelry of the libertine is short-lived
    and an irreligious man has only a momentary joy?
 6 Though he may achieve great eminence
    and attain lofty heights,
 7 he will follow his own dung downward.
    Those who watched him will ask, "Where is he?"
 8 He will fly away without a trace, like a dream,
    vanish like a vision of the night.
 9 He is mere appearance without substance,
    without a permanent place in the whole.
10 His sons will beg from the poor;
    his hands must return his gain.
11 While vigor still quickens his body,
    he will accompany it into the dust.

12 Though the fruit of evil is sweet in his mouth,
   and he hides it beneath his tongue,
13 loathe to let it go,
   holding it tight in his teeth,
14 his food turns sour in his stomach,
   becomes snake-poison in his intestine.
15 Though he swallows rich food, he will vomit.
   God will expel it from his gut.
16 He must suck on the bitter juice
   until its poison overcomes him.
17 He will not taste streams of oil,
   brooks of honey and butter,
18 nor consume the return from his toil
   nor enjoy the profit of his trading,
19 for he has broken into the toil of the poor,
   robbed the house which he did not build.
20 Because his appetite knows no satisfaction,
   he will not escape with what he desires,
21 there will be nothing left for him to eat,
   and his good life will not last.
22 When he reaches the zenith of abundance
   he will succumb to his fate,
   be exposed to the full force of failure.
23 To fill his belly, God will serve him fire,
   feed him flame for bread.
24 He will be routed by steel weapons
   and bronze arrowheads will pierce him.
26 Utter darkness lies in wait for him.
   An unfanned flame will consume him.
   Survivors left to him will be devoured.
27 The heavens will expose his guilt
   and the earth will be hostile to him.
28 His household possessions will be pilfered
   and carried off on the day of reckoning.
29 This is what a man of evil inherits,
   the estate decreed for him by God.

21:1   **Job**

 2 Now hear me out!
   Comfort me with listening.
 3 Bear with me while I speak.
   After I finish, you may resume your sport.

4 Do I address my complaint to man?
  Why shouldn't I be impatient?
5 Look me in the face!
  Take offense if you must,
  put your hands over your mouths.
6 When I think of it, even I am terrified,
  and chills attack my backbone.
7 Why is an evil man allowed to live?
  To reach old age? Even to accumulate wealth?
8 Why, his sons are set up in his business,
  and he watches them strike root with his own eyes.
9 His house is completely safe from fear—
  No "acts of God" destroy it.
10 His bull breeds without fail,
   and his heifers calve and never throw a calf.
11 He sends his children out to play like lambs,
   and they skip and dance before him.
12 He and his family play the tambourine and lyre
   and sing to the sound of the flute.
13 He lives the good life all his days
   and dies peacefully in his sleep.
14 Yet he says to God, "Leave us be!
   We don't want anything to do with You.
15 Why should we serve the deity?
   Can prayer to Him be cashed in?"
16 Now, isn't he master of his fortune?

24:1 Why doesn't Almighty God keep times of judgment?
    Why do the faithful never see His day of restitution?
  2 The scoundrel moves boundary markers,
    rustles flocks, and robs pasturage.
  3 He confiscates the orphan's mule
    and forecloses on a widow's cow.
  4 He runs the poor people off the road
    and frightens the wretched of the earth into hiding.
  9 He snatches the fatherless child from the breast
    and takes a poor man's infant in pledge.

 12 The shriek of the dying rises from the city
    and the throats of the wounded cry for help,
    but God pays no heed to their lamentation.
 22 Yet He preserves those in power by His grace.
    They rise up when they had despaired of life.
 23 He provides them with security and support
    and watches over them.
 25 Is it not so? Who then will charge me with lying?
    Who will refute my thesis?

45

21:17 How often, really, is the lamp of the oppressor extinguished?
How often does his scheming boomerang?
How often does God distribute suffering equitably?
18 How often is a villain straw caught by the wind?
Or chaff whipped away by a whirlwind?
19 "God sets aside punishment for his sons."
He should settle with the man himself.
20 Let his own eyes witness his downfall.
Let him drink God's wrath himself.
21 What does he care about his house,
once his own life is spent?

23 One dies with a feeling of fulfillment,
tranquil and contented,
24 blessed with prosperity,
health and vitality.
25 Another dies in utter disappointment,
having never tasted the good life.
26 They lie down together in the dust
and worms clothe both of them alike.

27 O yes, I know that you have clever rebuttals
and are devising ways to assault my position.
28 You will ask, "Where is the house of the tyrant?
Where has an oppressor's estate survived?"
29 Have you never talked with the merchants and pilgrims
who pass through our region on the highway?
You cannot reject their testimony

30 that on the day of calamity it is the opportunist who is spared,
he is the one who escapes when wrath breaks out.
31 And who ever describes his immorality to his face
or repays him in kind for what he does?
32 When he dies, he is borne to the grave,
and his tomb keeps watch over him.
33 Before and after his casket
marches a great funeral procession
and even the clods of the valley are pleasant to him.

34 How can you comfort me with abstractions?
Do your arguments still hold any weight?

Eliphaz the Temanite

2 Does God need human help?
    Isn't a man's intelligence to be used for his own good?
3 Has the Almighty shown delight in your righteousness?
    Has there been a reward for your perfect conduct?
4 Is it for your piety that He reproves you
    and enters into judgment with you?
5 Is it not for your utter corruption
    and endless series of sins?

6 You've foreclosed on loans to your brothers
    and stripped the clothing off the naked.
7 You have ignored the thirst of the weary
    and refused to give bread to the hungry.
8 You're a powerful man who owns the countryside
    and enjoys special privileges.
9 You have sent the widow away empty
    and cracked the arms of the orphan.
10 So now you walk in a maze of traps,
    and panic has suddenly dazed you.
11 Your eyes cannot penetrate the fallen darkness,
    and the onrushing flood drowns you.

12 Is not God high in heaven?
    Look above the most distant stars!
13 So you say, "What does God know of earthly affairs?
    How can He judge through the dark cloud?
14 He is shrouded in darkness; He cannot see.
    He walks about on the vault of heaven."
15 Will you too follow this crooked path
    which all worthless men walk?
16 They are snatched away before their time,
    their foundations washed away by the flood.
17 For they say to God, "Depart from us!
    What can the deity do for us?"
18 Yet it is he who fills their houses with every good thing.
19 When honest men observe them,
    they can take quiet comfort,
    they can chuckle to themselves:
20 "Aren't our enemies about to fall,
    and all that would remain after them to burn up?"

21 Sue for peace with Him, Job, surrender,
    and your fortunes will be reversed.
22 My friend, receive guidance from his mouth,
    adopt his words as a rule of life.
23 If you return to God and humble yourself
    and dissociate yourself from every evil,

26 Almighty God will become your sole joy,
   and you will stand erect before Him.
27 When you make a request of Him, He will grant it,
   and you can fulfill your vows in thanksgiving.
28 Whatever you choose to ask will be secured,
   and light will dawn upon your pursuits.
29 For He humbles those who exalt themselves
   and saves those with downcast eyes.
30 He delivers the innocent man,
   you yourself if your hands are clean.

27:5 God forbid that I ever declare you right!
     Until death I will not relinquish my claim of innocence!
  6 I will insist upon my integrity,
     hold it fast in this fist and never relax my grip,
     for my conscience does not reproach me for one day of my life!

23:3 O that I knew where to find Him
     that I might come before His throne.
  4 I would lay my case before Him
     and fill my mouth with arguments.
  5 I would learn His rebuttal
     and memorize His reasoning.
  6 Would He refute me by brute force?
     No, He would give me a fair hearing.
  7 There a man of integrity can argue with Him.
     I would be acquitted forever by my Judge.
 10 For He knows the way of my going.
     If He tried me by ordeal,
     I would come through it like gold.
 11 My foot follows fast in His footstep,
     and I do not deviate from His path.
 12 I do not stray from His directions,
     I have committed His words to heart.

 13 But if He has arrived at His decision,
     who can reverse it?
     He is free to do His arbitrary whim.
 14 So He will finish off my decreed destiny.
     He probably has more tortures in mind.

15 How terrified I am by His presence!
   The very thought of Him strings me up!
16 God has made me weak-willed,
   He has made me dumb with terror.
17 Am I not enveloped by darkness
   and my way concealed from me in gloom?

Narrator

27:11 Let me teach you of the hand of God.
      I will not conceal what He has at His disposal.
   12 Indeed all of you already know.
      Why then do you live with such cheap thoughts?

28:1 There is a place where silver is found
     and a site where gold is refined.
   2 Iron is extracted from the dust
     and copper is smelted from stone.
   3 Men sink shafts into the dark recesses
     and explore the bowels of the earth for ore
     in gloom and shadow.

4 They bore tunnels far below the surface,
  to places untouched by feet,
  hanging below, swinging back and forth on ropes.
5 Out of the earth comes a harvest;
  the underground is gutted out as if burnt by fire.
6 Its stones are the home of sapphire and gold dust.

7 The vulture does not know the way
  nor has the eye of the hawk spied it.
8 The wild animals have not trodden it;
  the lion has not passed over it.
9 Man alone chisels at flint rocks
  and turns up mountains by the roots.
10 He cuts channels in the rock,
  and his eyes fall on rare splendors.
11 He probes the very sources of rivers
  and brings an underground store to light.
12 But where can wisdom be found?
  Where is the deposit of understanding?
13 Man does not know the path to it,
  for it is not to be found in the land of the living.
14 And the deep says, "It is not in me."
  The sea says, "Not here."
15 It cannot be purchased with gold
  nor does it have a price measured in silver.
16 It cannot be put on the scales with the gold of Ophir,
  or precious onyx or sapphire.
17 It cannot be assessed in terms of gold and crystal,
  nor exchanged for gold jewelry,
18 not to mention coral or glass—
  The value of wisdom exceeds any precious thing.
19 No, not even Ethiopian topaz
  or pure gold is on the same scale.

20 But where, then, is the source of wisdom?
  Where is the deposit of understanding?
21 It is hidden from the eyes of every living creature,
  concealed from the birds of the sky,
22 and the underworld admits:
  "We have only heard of it by ear."
23 God alone knows the way to it
  and has knowledge of its hiding place.
24 When He surveyed the full expanse of the earth,
  inspecting everything under the skies,
25 and weighed the wind
  and measured the waters,
26 when He set the standard for the rain
  and gave the lightning and thunder their vocation,

27 He examined it too and wrote down its value,
   He studied it; He scrutinized it minutely.

2 O that my now were like the months of then,
   like the days of God's care,
3 when His lamp shone over my head
   and I walked in darkness by His light,
4 when I was in my fruitful years,
   when God was the shelter of my tent,
5 when the Almighty still went my way
   and my children surrounded me,
6 when my treading feet bathed in wine
   and my press squeezed out streams of oil.

7 When I went out to the city gate
   and took my seat in its chamber,
8 the young men saw me and stepped back,
   and the elders rose and stood,
9 nobles stopped in the middle of their speeches
   and put their hands to their lips,
10 the voice of the leaders went silent,
   and their tongues stuck to the roofs of their mouths.

21 They listened and waited,
   and a hush went over them when I gave advice.
22 After I spoke no one dissented
   for my words were completely persuasive.
23 They depended on me as one waits for rain
   and welcomes a shower with tongue out.
24 I smiled upon those who were not sure,
   and they could not resist the radiance of my face.
25 I chose their policy and sat at the head,
   enthroned like a monarch among his troops.
11 Every ear had heard of my conduct and was pleased,
   and every eye observed and attested
12 that I had delivered the poor when they cried for help,
   the fatherless and the helpless.
13 I received the blessing of the one who was failing
   and lifted the widow's heart.
14 I wore rectitude like clothing and it covered me,
   my just dealings were my robe and turban.

15 I was the eyes of the blind
   and the feet of the crippled.
16 I was a father to the weak
   and defended the cause of utter strangers.
17 I would break the bite of the oppressor
   and force him to drop his victim from his teeth.
18 So I thought to myself, "I shall die in old age,
   I shall live as many days as there are grains of sand.
19 My roots have burrowed to the water,
   and I'm refreshed by the dew of night.
20 My honor will continue to thrive,
   my potency will grow with effort."

30:1 But now I am jeered by young hoodlums
   whose fathers I would have disdained
   to set over the sheep dogs guarding my flock.
 2 Why would I have wanted their service,
   for they'd lost their vigor?
 3 They are gaunt from poverty and hunger,
   grubbing about the desolate, deserted steppe,
 4 picking mallow and bush-leaves
   and digging broom roots to burn.
 5 They are driven from settled areas,
   chased out like a thief,
 6 forced to live in wadi crevices,
   in caves hollowed out of the dirt and cliff.
 7 From a scrub-clump comes wild squeals and grunts;
   there they are huddled together.
 8 Such a despicable race, they even go without names.
   They are whipped out of the land.
 9 Yet now I am mocked in their songs,
   I've become a joke among them.
10 They treat me as an untouchable,
   and do not hesitate to spit in my face.
11 They undo my belt to humiliate me
   and throw away all restraint in my presence.

12 A mob amasses on my right,
   chases me along a road,
   blocks my way of escape,
13 and cuts off the foot path I pursue.
   They seek to destroy me,
   no friend among them—
14 they spill through a wide gap
   and swarm forth in waves, roaring.
15 He has turned terrors loose on me!
   My freedom is pursued like the wind,
   my future floats away like a cloud.

16 And now I've been drained of life,
    and days of misery lie ahead.
17 Night hollows out my bones.
    My pulsing pain takes no rest.
18 He jerks violently at my robe,
    grabs hold of my tunic collar,
19 and shoves me into the mud,
    and I take the semblance of dirt and dust.

20 I cry to You for help, but You do not answer me!
    I stand up, but You take no notice of me!
21 You have turned cruel to me.
    You have cuffed me with Your bare hand.
22 You have mounted me on the wind and made me ride
    and tossed me about upon a wild storm.
23 I now know that You will bring me death,
    the appointment facing every living thing.

24 Yet, doesn't a sinking man reach out his hand
    and cry for help in his distress?
25 Didn't I weep for the hard-time guy
    and show sympathy for the poor?
26 So I expected good, and evil came,
    anticipated light and got darkness.
27 My guts boil and burn,
    days of despair get the jump on me.

28 I go about darkened, but not by the sun.
   I rise in the congregation screaming for help.
29 I am a brother of the howling jackals
   and fit company for screeching ostriches.
30 My skin blackens and peels
   and my bones burn with heat.
31 My harp plays only dirges
   and my flute accompanies weeping.

27:2 I swear by the living God,
   who has robbed me of right,
   who has poisoned my spirit,
3 that as long as there is breathing in my chest,
   a breath of Life in my nose,
4 my lips will not speak falsely
   nor will my tongue utter perjury.
31:6 Let God weigh me on the scales of justice
   and discover my integrity!

31:1 I have imposed a ban on my eyes
   never to gaze at a ripe virgin.
2 If I succumbed, what would be my reward from God above,
   my inheritance from the exalted Lord?
3 What but the misery destined for sinful men?
   The shocks in store for nihilists?
4 Does God not see my conduct
   and count all my steps?

5 If ever I followed a devious course
   or my foot rushed for a chance at fraud,
7 if I have deviated but a step,
   or let my heart follow my eyes
   or stained my hands,
8 let me sow and another eat
   and let my planting be uprooted.

38 If my land has accused me
   and its furrows have sought restitution,
39 if I have eaten its strength without replenishment
   and exhausted the powers of the soil,
40 let thistles come up instead of wheat,
   weeds instead of barley.

9 If my heart was ever seduced by a woman
   and I skulked to my neighbor's door,
10 let my own wife be laid by another,
   let strangers cuckold me,
11 for I would have committed adultery,
   a serious breach of morality,
12 a fire burning even beyond death
   and raging through all I have gained.

13 If I have been contemptuous of the claim of my slave
or my maid's suit against me,
14 what will I do when God is aroused,
how will I reply to His inquiry?
15 Isn't my Creator his also?
Isn't He who fashioned us one?
16 If I've refused to fill the needs of the poor
or the wants of a widow,
17 if I ate my meal alone
and did not share it with a fatherless boy—
18 All my life I've been a father to orphans—
19 if I have seen someone freezing for lack of clothing
or an impoverished person forced to go naked,
20 and he did not bless me
for warming him with lamb's wool,
21 if I have accused one of the disadvantaged
because I saw accomplices among the judges in the gate,
22 let my shoulder be separated from my neck
and my arm be snapped from its socket.
23 For I have feared God's judgment,
nor could I have endured His majesty.

24 If I have put faith in gold
and said to fine gold, "I place my trust in you,"
25 if I have taken pride in my wealth
or in being a self-made man,
26 if I looked at the shining sun
or the moon circling in splendor,
27 and my heart was secretly seduced
and I made a gesture of worship with my hand,
28 I would have committed serious sins,
having been disloyal to the transcendent God.

29 If I have rejoiced at the ruin of an enemy,
celebrated when hard luck found him—
30 I have never allowed my mouth to sin
by requesting his life in prayer—
31 if the persons of my household did not say,
"Who is there who is not filled with meat?"—
32 The stranger did not have to sleep in the street,
for I always opened my doors to the traveler—
33 if I have concealed crimes from men,
hidden my guilt in my memory,
34 may I become terrified of gatherings of people,
seized by fear of ostracism from the members of my clan,
so that I retire and do not venture out-of-doors.

35 How I wish He had heard me!
Here is my X! Now let God reply!
Let my opponent write an indictment!

36 I would be proud to wear it on my shoulder
   or strap it on my head like a crown.
37 I would stride before Him as a noble before his king
   and give an account of my every step.

38:1   **The Lord**

(from the Whirlwind)

2 Who is this who muddles the discussion
   by words without knowledge?
3 Take your stand like a man!
   I will interrogate you and you will testify!

4 Were you there when I founded the world?
   Speak out if you possess the knowledge!
5 Who drew up its measurements?
   Who stretched out a measuring-tape over the site?
6 To what were its piles sunk?
   Who laid its cornerstone
7 while the morning stars sang together
   and the heavenly beings chanted joyfully?

8 Were you there when the sea was shut off by floodgates
   as it came bursting forth from its source?
9 When I clothed it with clouds
   and covered it with deep blue?
10 When I decreed its extent,
   put it behind walls and gates,
11 and told it: "Come thus far and no farther!
   Here your high swells shall break!"

12 Have you ever commanded the morning,
   given the dawn its orders
13 to leap to the extremes of the earth
   and drive its occupants into the open?
14 The world is changed like clay under a seal,
   dyed dapple like a robe,
15 and just as quickly robbed of light,
   while people are still at work.

16 Have you prowled the sources of the sea
   or explored the depths of the deep?
17 Have the gates of death been shown you?
   Have you inspected the archway to the dark land?

18 Have you mapped the outer regions?
Detail the features, if you happen to know.
19 Where is the road to the home of light?
Where is darkness located?
20 Can you take them to their spheres?
Trace the paths to their domains?
21 You would know if you were born then,
if your life had spanned the ages.

22 Have you checked the supplies of snow
or seen the stock of hail
23 held in reserve for bad seasons
when nature wages war?
24 Where can you find the distribution center for the wind?
Where is the hot east wind released from?

25 Who regulates the flow of torrential rain
and directs the flight of the thunderbolt,
26 and channels the rainfall even to places where no human lives,
to uninhabited deserts and peaks,
27 to soak the lonely waste
and sprout the plants of the dry soil?

28 Does the rain have a sire?
Who are the parents of the dew?
29 Whose issue is the ice?
To which dam can you trace the hoarfrost
30 which hardens water to stone
and freezes the surface of deep water?

31 Did you forge together the links of the Pleiades?
Can you untie the cords linking Orion?
32 Can you dispatch the signs of the Zodiac season by season?
Can you guide the Great Bear with its cubs?
33 Do you know the laws of heavenly bodies?
Can you establish their influence upon earth?

34 Can you raise up your voice to the clouds
and bring down a shower of rain?
35 Does lightning obey your orders?
Will it say to you: "Yes sir!"
36 Who has implanted wisdom in the elements
and taught the weather a pattern?
37 Who measures the cloud cover in wisdom?
Who pours out the suspended water tanks
38 when the ground hardens to cast iron
and the clouds pack together?

39 Do you hunt game for the lion
and satisfy the hunger of young lions

57

40 when they crouch in their dens
and lie impatiently in their lairs?
41 Who provides prey to the raven
when its young scream to God
and wander about for lack of food?

39:1 Do you inform the mountain goat when to kid?
Do you watch over the calving of the hind?
2 Do you count out their gestation periods?
Do you set the date of birth,
3 the hour when they squat down, their wombs open,
and they drop their young?
4 Their offspring grow strong and healthy in the wild
and leave their parents and do not return.

5 Who grants the wild ass its freedom?
Who sets it loose from halter and harness?
6 Who adapts it to the steppe
and houses it on the open range?
7 It scorns the bustling town
and does not hear the shouting driver.
8 It ranges the mountains for its pasture
and scours the countryside for any green plant.

19 Do you furnish the horse with spirit?
Do you send quivers through his neck?
20 Do you make him leap like a grasshopper?
Make him snort majestically at fear?
21 He paws at the ground and lunges
forward to meet the weapons.
22 He shows disdain for terror;
he does not shy from close combat
23 with arrows, lances, and javelins
whizzing by over him.
24 He eats up the ground amidst noise and confusion.
He cannot stand still when the bugle blows.
25 At its blast he says, "Aha!"
sniffing the battle at a distance,
the thunder of captains and war cries.

26 Is it by your wisdom that the hawk soars
and spreads its wings for the south?
27 Does the eagle mount up
and nest at such heights at your word?
28 It makes its home on the cliff
and perches upon the cliff crag.
29 From there it scans the horizon for prey,
watching for any movement in miles.

40:2 Will this critic continue to dispute with the deity?
Let the one who accuses God answer these questions!

3 **Job**

4 O, I am too small!
What could I say to You?
I plead silence.
5 Once I spoke, but I cannot reply;
twice, but I cannot continue.

6 **The Lord**

(from the whirlwind)

7 Take your stand like a man!
I will interrogate you and you will testify!
8 Will you really impugn My justice?
Condemn Me to prove your innocence?

9 Do you have an arm like a god?
Can you thunder with a voice like one?
10 Adorn majesty and splendor,
attire yourself in grandeur and glory!
11 Mete out your restless wrath!
Survey every human majesty and humble it,
12 survey every exalted ruler and subdue him,
and stamp despots beneath your feet.
13 Bury them in the dirt,
wrap their faces in shrouds!

14 Then even I will sing your praises
for you will have proven
that you have the power to save yourself.

41:1 Can you pull Leviathan up
from the ocean depths with a hook?
Strap down his tongue with a line?
2 Slip a hemp noose over his snout?
Poke a gaff-hook through his jaws?
3 Will he pour out his supplications to you?
Move you to hear him with flattery?
4 Will he make a contract with you?
Can you force him to be your lifelong slave?
5 Can you play with him like a pet bird
or leash him like a peacock for your maidens?
7 Can you plant harpoons in his hide
or fishing spears in his head?
8 Just lay your hand upon him!
Think of the battle! You won't do it twice!
9 Any hope of conquest is empty.
Has not the very sight of him defeated gods?

10 No man is so courageous as to arouse him.
Who then can take his stand before Me?
11 Who has confronted Me and survived?
Who under the broad sky?

42:1 **Job**

2 Now I know that You can do it all!
Nothing You propose can be thwarted!
3 Therefore I declare—though I do not understand!—
wonders beyond me—though I do not comprehend!
5 I had heard of You by the word of others,
but now I have encountered You in person.
6 Therefore I repudiate and forswear
dust and ashes.

Narrator

7   After the Lord had finished speaking to Job, He said to Eliphaz
the Temanite: "I am hot with anger against you and your two friends
because you have not spoken truthfully of Me, as did My servant
8 Job. So you are to take seven bulls and seven rams and go to My
servant Job. Offer up the bulls and rams in your own behalf and My

60

servant Job will make intercession for you. I will accept his entreaty
not to act foolishly toward you, though you did not speak truthfully

9 of Me, as did my servant Job." And Eliphaz the Temanite, Bildad
the Shuhite, and Zophar the Naamathite went and did what the
Lord had told them to do. And the Lord accepted Job's entreaty.

10 And the Lord turned Job's fortunes when he prayed in behalf
of his friends. And the Lord returned everything to Job which
he once had twice over.

11 All his brothers and sisters and former friends visited him
and ate bread with him in his house, and offered him sympathy
and comfort for the many misfortunes the Lord had burdened him
with, and each one gave him a valuable coin and a gold ring.

12 Then the Lord blessed Job's later years even more than He had
his earlier years. He amassed fourteen thousand sheep, six thousand

13 camels, a thousand yoke of oxen, and a thousand she-asses. He had

14 seven sons and three daughters. He named the first daughter Jemi-
mah, he named the second Keziah, and he named the third Keren-

15 Happuch. No women could be found in all the land as beautiful as
Job's daughters, and their father gave them an inheritance in the

16 midst of their brothers. After this, Job lived one hundred and forty
years and saw his children and grandchildren to the fourth genera-

17 tion. Job died old and fulfilled.

How to Read
the Chapters That Follow

When I began talking to Sherman Hanson, the editor of Bethany Press, about a book on Job, he convinced me that a translation was not enough. The most important part of such a book must be a discussion of the meaning of Job and the lessons it may have for us who live in the twentieth century. The reason for books about the Bible is to help the modern reader understand and respond to the Scriptures. I am to be your guide into the familiar yet strange new world of the Bible.

When I sat down to write, I found it difficult to write in a style and at a level that would appeal to the general reader. A virtual tome of dull pages piled up on the editor's desk before I hit upon the idea of composing a chapter as if I were Job. Once I thought myself into the person of Job, imagining what he would tell someone about his experience, the proper tone and style appeared almost automatically.

So my first interpretive chapter is composed as if Job were reflecting on what has happened to him. One is to imagine Job sitting in the gate of his city talking to his fellow elders a decade or so later. In a real sense, though, he is talking directly to us.

From time to time Job addresses God personally. This is what he did in the drama, and I wanted to preserve the same spirit. Job feels God's presence so vividly that he can turn and address the unseen party as if He were sitting with Him. To make it clear when God is being addressed, the "You" has been capitalized. When Job refers to God in third person, "He" is capitalized.

Job's explanation of his story is my interpretation of his experience. Into it I pour all my thoughts on the drama. My Job recreates how he felt about his friends, what he thought about God, how he saw his own situation. He explains why he said what he did and then offers what he now thinks after God has spoken to him. Hopefully you can enjoy my imaginary Job and gain insight into the original at the same time.

The three chapters that follow Job's explanation of his story are written in the same casual, down-to-earth style, but now in my own name. Each is devoted to an aspect of the drama of Job. The first highlights Job's prayer and offers some food for the reader's thought about his or her own prayer life. What role should prayer play in our lives? Should prayer be an honest expression of how we feel? Can we expect an answer to our prayer?

The second of the three interpretive chapters explains how the Book of Job refutes the doctrine that God rewards the righteous and punishes the wicked. Job is an example of a person who suffers without deserving God's punishment. If the righteous suffer and the wicked prosper, why should we be righteous? If death erases the distinction between good and evil, why do we struggle so with our consciences? Is there any hope for those who place their fate in the hands of God?

The final interpretive chapter reflects on the identity of the God who addresses Job from the whirlwind. Job's is a story of God's redemption of His good name. He must convince Job that He is worthy of Job's praise. How does God show Job that He is not a hostile tyrant, but the righteous Creator from whom Job must seek salvation? What does He say about creation that makes Job see it in a new light? How does He show Job that His awe-inspiring power works to Job's benefit?

My interpretive chapters are not the final word on the meaning of Job. You will probably see things differently than I do. A work like Job is too fertile for any one mind. Indeed, its greatness lies in the fact that it is as complex and many sided as life itself. The questions with which this book deals do not have pat answers. We are engulfed in mysteries and enigmas that await the last judgment for clarification. The best we can do in this life is tell stories that celebrate God's presence among us.

I have included an appendix for the curious or puzzled reader who wants to know why some chapters are left out, others are out of order, and why my translation of a verse diverges from the standard translations of the Bible. I try to explain the judgments I made as a scholar.

Job Explains His Own Story

The proverb runs, "the patience of Job," but nothing could be further from the truth. The truth is, I refused to abandon my integrity, and that's what got me my hearing from God. Legend has it that I was tested by God. Really, though, it was God who was on trial. I challenged Him to answer for His actions and He responded. Now let me explain.

Let's start from the beginning. According to legend, I had all of my possessions and children taken from me, and I myself was afflicted with boils. True, all too true. The part about the Lord's deal with Satan is—well, I'm not sure God has to answer to anyone; I'm not convinced that He has to test us to know whether we are honest in our integrity. Who knows where the story came from? I certainly did not know why all these things had happened to me. How can we know what is going on in heaven?

I Accepted My Affliction

At first I accepted my affliction. The Giver of life, I thought to myself, has the right to take it away when He pleases. How can the vessel complain to the potter about what it is made into? But wait—that is dangerous reasoning, it would allow God to be a tyrant. If God commands us to be just, shouldn't He be? But I didn't raise these questions until my friends Eliphaz, Bildad, and Zophar joined me on the ash heap. Yes, it was these friends who provoked me. I became a different person!

Those companions! Some friends they were! I came to realize that they were really my enemies . . . my persecutors. God had sent them to break my will (or so I thought until He revealed Himself to me). Well, they meant to comfort me, it's just that they were misled by their zeal for God's righteousness. Yes, it was their belief that God always acts justly that turned them into persecutors and false witnesses.

You know how they thought: If God is just, our suffering must be punishment. Everything God does is right, so we ourselves are to blame for every misfortune. All of us, they said, are sinners, so any time that God decides to punish us, we deserve it. In fact, we always deserve more than we actually receive, because God is gracious. But there is a hope: If a person is basically good and properly humbles himself when God punishes him, God will reverse his fate and lift him up again to his rightful place. That's the gist of what they were saying and repeating over and over again.

They've got you coming and going. It's hard to deny that we're all sinners. We always feel filthy and corrupt in the presence of God. There are always things that could be dredged up against us. Who isn't guilty of a nasty thought now and then? We're always at a severe disadvantage when we propose to protest against God's punishment. It seems so much easier to submit humbly, confess that we received what we deserved (or even less than we deserve) and cry for mercy.

God Takes Advantage of our Shame and Guilt

It occurred to me that God takes advantage of our sense of shame and guilt. He silences our protest against His injustice—the suffering of the innocent and righteous and the success of the ruthless and powerful. The sensitive person is all too willing to admit his wrongs and accept his punishment. God is never called to account. I had to fight back my conscience to make the protest I did—I could feel God's eyes penetrating my heart and recording every false move. But that was unfair intimidation—it was silencing me. The righteous always feel God's glance, but the wicked don't seem to.

Well, my friends really could not bear my refusal to submit. They became harsher and harsher as time went on. To them what I was saying was blasphemy, and they sought to scare me into silence. You know, Eliphaz admitted that I was a righteous man when he first addressed me, but when he spoke the third time he condemned me for committing every wicked and impious deed known to man!

How did this change come about? Why would men who knew my righteousness come to make such charges? Men who knew me as a friend and wished me well. They refused to witness to my righteousness before God (as I had hoped they would) and finally uttered lies against me!

You know as well as I do what happened. They felt they had to defend the honor of God. When I accused God of evil, they were sure that I was evil, for only an evil person could say such horrible things. Their God was too small; he had to be protected; all detractors had to be silenced. If truth had to be sacrificed, so be it.

My refutation of their dogmas provoked Eliphaz's false charges. I was making my argument, he reasoned, to cover up the fact that I was suffering God's judgment for wickedness. His secure little universe was more important than truth to him.

I Argue with God About Prayer

As I say, I refused to debate with them most of the time. My dispute was with God. Indeed, my real conflict with Eliphaz, Bildad, and Zophar was over the proper way to pray. Yes, there can be a conflict over the proper way to pray. I insisted on the right to express my dismay and anger at God for turning against me. I insisted on accusing God of betraying me and condemning me without a fair trial. In a word, I insisted on telling it like it was. My companions believed that it was irreligious to blame God for one's troubles.

Lord, it was not easy for me to speak to You. At first all I could do was curse the day of my birth and avoid thinking of You. Then slowly I worked up the courage to address You. But once I was able to open up, all my feelings began pouring out. You had become my enemy. I was no threat to Your rule of the world, but You were (or seemed to be) treating me as if I were. Why do You keep us under surveillance and punish us every time we step out of line? Aren't You powerful enough to tolerate our follies?

And then Bildad attacked me for not admitting my guilt. No creature, he assured me, can presume to be perfect or righteous before God. I had to agree that the cards are stacked against us. If I tried to prove my innocence, I was afraid that God would condemn me anyway. Since He was the judge, how could I be sure of a fair hearing? To admit my innocence would be to admit His mistake—and God can't make mistakes! But what difference does innocence make? Experience shows that the innocent suffer right along with the guilty, if not more so.

But I knew I had to challenge His decision, even if it meant my death. Mine was to be a test case. I would stand up to Him in behalf of all who suffer innocently. I would demand that my case be re-opened, that You defend the action You had taken against me. I knew that You knew my integrity. You must, I thought, have a sadistic streak. You create us and encourage us to trust in You, then suddenly turn against us. Why? Why?

Let no one be mistaken. I never lost my belief in the power of God. No, God was all too powerful for me. I knew that He controlled nature and determined our destinies. But the power of God still terrifies me! He seems so often to be out to destroy us. Again and again I have seen nations and leaders thrown from their positions of power. It makes me shudder to contemplate the tragedies I have witnessed. Anyone who tries to make morality plays out of these tragedies is deceived, lying to protect the honor of God. It simply isn't right to lie on behalf of God and God himself will condemn anyone who does.

My One Hope

I had one hope, one very slim hope: That God would hear the pleas of the innocent and righteous but refuse to hear those of the guilty. Perhaps I would get a hearing and have my integrity confirmed. I was afraid that He might kill me for my impertinence or simply overwhelm me by His majesty, but I hoped that He would prove just and loving. O what contradictory things I said! I felt! I was appealing to the justice of the very One I was condemning for injustice! To the benevolence of the very One I felt had turned cruel!

When the time came to challenge Him, I simply asked for an explanation, nothing more, nothing mysterious. I simply wanted the grounds of Your verdict. Were You digging up some terrible sin out of my past? Why, why had You condemned me? Couldn't You re-open the case and let me defend myself? I knew that I was innocent and only needed a fair trial.

The Possibility of Death Without Reconciliation

Life seemed so horrible in those hours. It seemed that I suddenly discovered conclusive proof that all our striving is futile. Yes, life had been good to me, but my fall from fortune made it all seem like a mean joke. More than anything it is death that stalks us. Life is always running out; we are plunging toward the grave; there is no pause. And there is utterly no hope in the grave; it is dark and terrifying, the enemy of hope and life.

What if I died before we were reconciled? Could I wait in the underworld until You were ready to meet me? Preposterous! When one is dead, there's nothing for You to address! You've got to act in time or all is lost. How many, many people have gone to the grave without knowing Your consolation? Lord, don't You see that death is evil? Why must we be tortured with it?

When You did not reply to my challenge and my companions began to bear down even harder, I lost my capacity to pray. I almost gave up speaking altogether. If I'd stopped, my cause would have been lost completely. I don't know what kept me going. Nothing I said seemed to make any difference. You had become so foreign and mean to me that I could only address You now and then, and I finally gave up entirely. You were my enemy. You showed no mercy. How lonely I was!

What kept me going was this crazy hope—not really crazy, but impossible, inconceivable—I hoped that despite my death we would be reconciled. I came to believe, or rather to hope against hope, that somewhere in the supernatural world someone would testify in my behalf after He had killed me. Even if God himself must be brought to justice, so be it! I did not know who might be my advocate, I only knew that God himself would have to submit to the scrutiny of justice. God himself would have to admit that He'd murdered me. Perhaps You would act as my advocate Yourself—against Yourself.

The first time I explored this hope, I could not really believe it. Death would silence me and there would be no one to redeem my name after all. I would not be around to insist upon my rights. Death would wipe away all evidence of my existence.

But the second time, I overcame my fears. My death, I decided, would precipitate an inquiry. My words would be recorded and a vindicator would testify to my innocence. Who would testify for me? I don't know. Perhaps God, perhaps another. All I knew was that my case would not be buried with me, that justice would prevail, that my protest would not have been in vain. Once I was vindicated, God would no longer despise me. He would seek me out and I would experience it—yes, I would see my loving Creator again, though I was dead!

You say such ideas are crazy? You're wrong. I could not address the God who was attacking me. I could only await a God who appears after the eclipse, after his wrath had passed. If this meant after death, and I was sure that my death was necessary to provoke an inquiry—well God can perform the impossible. What kind of Creator would He be if He couldn't find us in death?

My Struggle Ends

In a way, my struggle with You ended at this point. I had accepted my death and given up hope of being reconciled with You before it. But history never ends at the logical point. It trails on, it forces itself on . . . God tears apart what He builds and then fulfills what He has seemingly discarded.

69

After Zophar's ugly recitation of the fate of the wicked, I could not hold my peace any longer. I had to descend to their level and tear apart their moralistic little universe. Eliphaz then charged me with oppression and godlessness. This was the last straw. I turned my back on them. If men are willing to distort the truth to fit their dogmas, are even willing to bear false witness, then a man of integrity can only rely on God. People can be so despicable when their religion is threatened!

Don't forget, God condemned Eliphaz, Bildad, and Zophar and forced them to seek my intercession. God said that they had not spoken of him in truth, as I had. Their doctrine was false because it forced them to close their minds to my claim of innocence and finally to make false charges against me. It was false because it forced them to defend God with falsehoods—and our God condemns falsehood. God is just in a much more mysterious way than their doctrine of rewards and punishments describes him.

God's answer was the strongest evidence of His justice. He did not condemn me for accusing Him, no, He came to me and overthrew any false idea that my suffering proved my guilt. Yes, he righted an injustice. He confirmed me in my integrity and rewarded my refusal to lie and surrender to tyranny. Indeed, He demonstrated that He was not a tyrant and did not approve a religion that made us servile subjects. May all who hear my story learn this lesson.

God Is Marvelous

What a marvelous God! Even Your belligerence and mistreatment of me—so mysterious and arbitrary—served the cause of justice and truth. You forced me to abandon my own false beliefs—for I shared the beliefs of my companions until I underwent this experience. You forced me to protest Your mistreatment and finally to rely on a wild hope. Now, I know that our world is shot through with injustice and that justice breaks in as hope against things as they are. We must protest things as they are. We are not guaranteed any reward for our righteousness, we have only the promise of Your approval. Your actions were just, precisely because they were unjust and forced me to await a justice in the future.

But I'm getting way ahead of myself. After my experience with my so-called friends I realized that justice and truth depend upon God. When the crunch comes, men will abandon you every time. They will lie to protect their cozy little universes or their own skins. If I had to depend upon the recognition of humans for my integrity, I would have been lost. But I knew that God was a trustworthy friend, if I could only find Him. Before God, I could present my defense and He would respect me. Yet, I could not overcome my fear that I would not gain access to God before He finished me off. Perhaps His decision was irreversible.

I do not know who wrote that beautiful poem about the hiddenness of wisdom, but it is a perfect commentary on my struggle with my companions and with God. We humans are very clever at finding and digging up precious metals. Yes, we are unique among God's creatures. We are indeed set apart from all other animals. But wisdom—that's another question! We can't find it anywhere; we can't buy it; all our cleverness is vain. Do we have an explanation for suffering? Do we know why there is evil in God's creation? Can we account for why things happen as they do? Don't all our answers lead to more questions? Don't we get dizzy and sick at the stomach pursuing them? Only God has access to wisdom. Why does He keep us in the dark? Why must we trust in His wisdom?

I Had a Clear Conscience

When all is said and done, the one and only certainty I had was my clear conscience. I knew that I was innocent and that God had no right to rob and plunder me and then demand my self-respect. Yes, He had the power to rob me and human lackies to persuade me to submit to Him. My external fate I had no control over, but my integrity I could stand up for.

How does one chart His way when He is hemmed in by darkness? He tries to remember his way; he mulls over the past; he reviews His story. I had received grace in abundance, my way was illumined by his lamp. What a shock it was to have it snuffed out! And His care had not been wasted on me. I had led my people in wisdom and delivered the poor and needy from oppressors. "Justice, justice you shall follow, that you may live and inherit the land." Lord, You turned cruel to me! I did follow justice, but You stripped me of honor and shoved me in the mud. Why?

I refused then and I would refuse again to lie about my innocence. To rest my case and challenge God to defend his action, I took an oath that I hadn't committed any serious offense in my life. I had not stolen or defrauded, or committed adultery, or exhausted my land, or rejected the pleas of the weak and afflicted, or trusted in idols, or wished my enemies ill. My life was exemplary! Let no man call me self-righteous! Would you rob a person of the right to self-respect? I am righteous and refuse to be cowered. I had—and have—a right to your respect and God's approval.

I hoped that my oath would provoke a reply from my judge, some indication that He cared about the fairness of His decisions. Just to know the nature of the charge against me would be a victory for truth. If my accusations had been out-of-bounds, let Him show me their falsehood. And He did. Yes, Lord, You broke Your silence and redeemed Your rule.

God Speaks to Me from the Whirlwind

What a day that was when He spoke to me from the whirlwind! It is the *fact* that You answered me that made the difference, not what You said. Your silence was broken. This was the saving event. You had come down from Your remote heights to meet me in my suffering. You had ceased showing me a frowning countenance and revealed Your incomprehensible favor. I had heard that You condescended to Your creatures, but not until that day did I know it to be true.

I did not expect You to bless me with Your presence, not really, despite what I had said. But I did expect that if You granted me an audience, You would ask me to defend my life, prove my righteousness. But You didn't ask me to do this; You did not dispute my claim to innocence. You confirmed my integrity by simply appearing to me.

But His revelation was hardly a comforting assurance of salvation! No, it contained a "no" as well as a "yes." He came to meet me in legal combat, in combat over the charges I had leveled against Him. He forced me to defend my accusations and proved that I didn't know whereof I spoke. Not to enlighten me—no, He didn't say anything I didn't know—not to enlighten me, but to force me to praise Him. Yes, that's it—He wrested my accusations from me and replaced them with praise.

It's all very simple. He exercised the right of the accused to cross-examine His accuser. First, He attacked my credibility. What can a mere man know? Was I present when the world was created? Have I inspected the mysteries of the world? Only God knows such things, for He created them. We humans can't know the whys and wherefores of creation because we were not its creators nor observers at creation. At most we can describe its operations from the outside.

He also forced me to admit my impotence. Do I command morning and night? Do I lead about the stars? Do I control the weather? Of course not. I don't have the power to create a providential order. I wouldn't know how, and nothing would obey me anyway. The order of things follows patterns dictated by someone else, no matter how we might dislike it.

He kept asking who this someone was—who drew up the measurements of the world, who regulates the weather, who provides the animals with food and offspring and instincts? Not I. The world into which I was born was already established. I did not design or make it, and it goes its own way without any human interference. We live in it, depend upon it, take it for granted, and adjust to it.

Not I, but God

No, we did not create the world, and we do not have the power and knowledge to control it, but You do. All of Your questions lead to praise. They all demand the answer: Not I, but God. It is You who erected the earth, confined the sea, command the day and night, survey the remote regions, order the weather, produce the seasons, take care of the beasts of the wild, grant freedom to the ass, spirit to the horse and the power of flight to the hawk.

I already knew these things. I had in fact brooded over Your overwhelming, even sinister power and wisdom. I felt such a God was inimical to us and to our fellow creatures. How could such a God be made to conform to rules of fair play?

His questions made me look at the world again, not for purpose and design, but as filled with wonder and beauty. What a poet He is! He kept forcing me to consider how I would create a universe. You made me think of building a house, then look up at the heavens and think about building them. How could I sink foundations into an empty void? What kind of carpenter did it take to make heaven and earth! Are light, darkness, rain, hail, and snow stored in warehouses? Of course not, but that's the way we humans would have to store them. It's the difference between our ways and God's that evokes the marvel of His activity.

Those animals He mentioned! How strange and sublime is His work! Not only does He care for these animals, He gave them odd and eccentric qualities simply for the love of variety. "Glory be to God for dappled things!" Who can but praise such a sublime artist and poet as Gerard Manley Hopkins?

I certainly couldn't continue to accuse You. You had not explained anything; You had not defended your actions; You had not demonstrated some hidden design that we could see if we simply knew more. You simply forced me to acknowledge that I am a creature, Your creature, no match for Your wisdom, power, and artistry.

But You weren't satisfied with my silence, my dumbness. You wanted me to acknowledge You not only as Creator but also as Lord of humanity and, therefore, our savior. So You resumed the cross-examination. This time You attacked the logic behind my accusations. Both I and my companions were caught in a dilemma: I could not be innocent if you were just. My claim to innocence forced me to accuse You of violating my rights, and my companions accused me of deeds deserving Your punishment. Neither of us was right. I cannot prove my innocence by condemning You, for we humans depend upon You to set the standard and decide the right.

His questions and challenges turned my attention toward the human world. Could I rule history? Could I overthrow the mighty and powerful? Although this would seem to be nearer my grasp, I would have to admit that I could no more overthrow the mighty than make the thunder obey my command.

The struggle to control our destiny and become our own saviors is the chief cause of our self-destructive activities. It is precisely what motivates us to become despots and oppressors. When we seek to rule history, we become the very persons and nations God overthrows in acts of judgment. Every attempt to rule ourselves produces the struggle for power with others which God must bring under check.

We Must Accept God's Sovereignty

We must accept His sovereign rule or suffer from it. Our only hope of salvation resides in Him, for He alone stands above the conflicts of men and has the power to overthrow the mighty and powerful. I brooded about the tragedies of human history earlier, and I will probably continue to brood over them, but I have no power to change our lot. Lord, You alone can save.

Confronting God seems so easy and harmless, much less dangerous than confronting a vicious beast—like Leviathan. But the opposite is the truth. If we are terrified by a creature, how much more terrifying must be his master! God's actions must overwhelm and destroy all opposition. Everything You do establishes Your power. How foolish I was to contemplate meeting You as an equal and defending my ways before You. Between us is an impassible gulf.

Yet You did not destroy me. Now I understand that Your power is not a threat to Your goodness. Now I know that You could have destroyed me but did not because You were free from the compulsion of defending Your power. You did not have to silence a just protest to assert Your power; You were free to hear me and acknowledge my righteousness. You are not like the parent who insists on asserting his or her authority, right or wrong, but like the parent who establishes authority by listening and rendering a just decision, even if it should mean admitting a wrong has occurred.

Did God explain to me why I had suffered? Why the innocent suffer? Can the solution to this age-old enigma now be announced to the world? No, not really. No, God did not defend what He had done; He did not explain a higher necesssity or economy; He did not beg off blame—rather He righted a wrong; He responded to my cries and changed my accusations into praise, my lamentation into rejoicing.

By the way, did you notice how I became reconciled to my friends? God judged between us and forced them to acknowledge their wrong and forced me to forgive and intercede for them. This is the role of the righteous: To intercede in behalf of their persecutors. God hears the prayers of those who have been victimized in behalf of their victimizers.

Prayer in a World of Action

The title of this chapter is a paraphrase of a beautiful book entitled *Contemplation in a World of Action* by a Catholic Trappist monk named Thomas Merton. Like Merton I believe that prayer and contemplation belong in a well-rounded, complete life. Job is an important lesson in the way life's tough questions and experiences are wrestled with and resolved in prayer. First let us reflect upon prayer in an active life and then look at Job's prayer.

To a modern, practical man or woman of affairs, prayer seems like wasted time. Why sit around and talk when there is something to do? Anyway, prayer seems so unproductive. If we are honest with ourselves, we will admit that we aren't quite sure that God is listening and will answer us.

The irony is that substitutes for prayer are being taken up by thousands upon thousands of Americans. Teaching Americans meditation has become a flourishing business for Indian holy men. It seems that we humans have a spiritual need for withdrawal from everyday activity and distraction. Our bodies need it for health; our minds and emotions need it for wholeness and creativity.

Prayer has the same physical and psychological effect upon us as meditation. It quiets us down and puts us in another mood and state of mind. We are removed from the petty pace of everyday life and feel "together" again.

Prayer Is at the Heart of Life

But prayer is different from meditation. It puts us in contact with God. It is more personal. We speak to God and wait on an answer.

Prayer is more demanding because it requires us to be committed. We can meditate without believing in anything. All we have to believe is that meditation is good for us. But prayer is another story. We must believe that God exists. We must believe that He is listening and can respond to our needs. We must open ourselves to His inspection, confess our guilt and inadequacy, and acknowledge that He knows more about us than we know about ourselves. Such honesty is sometimes hard.

Prayer is engagement with life. If God exists, He is the most important person in anyone's life. He is the very heart of life. When we enter into conversation with Him, we have moved from the periphery to the center. The story of our life is determined by Him, and the heart of that story is the conversation we carry on with Him.

If we are what God judges us to be and makes us into, prayer is crucial for finding ourselves. Prayer is indeed two-way communication. We discover our real selves when we sense the effect on the Holy One of what we say. There is a drama between our words and our feeling for how they are being received.

There is not only judgment and purgation, there is also encouragement and fortification in prayer. We find ourselves resolving to pursue a righteous course and to right wrongs we or others are perpetrating. We vow to fulfill our obligations to our friends and simply be more friendly. We vow to seek excellence in our vocation and overcome that thirst called ambition.

Prayer puts things in perspective. It is not what we think is important but what God thinks is important that determines the value of things. We discover that being a father and husband takes precedence over job advancement or even intellectual accomplishment. We also discover that the pursuit of excellence takes precedence over popularity, comfort, and excitement. From God's point of view we see things in a different light than we see them from our own, and it is God's perspective that prayer offers us. God reminds us, even nags us, about the important things of life.

Prayer comes into its own in times of crisis. It is in such times that we know we're in need of help, all the help that we can get from whatever quarter. As the saying goes, there are no atheists in foxholes. What greater source of help than the Lord of heaven and earth? To Him the nations of the earth are but drops in a bucket, yet He makes the tired and weary mount up with eagles' wings (Isa. 40:15-17, 29-31).

Are Prayers Answered?

But I hear you object: Does God really help? What of those who died in the foxholes? Why weren't their prayers answered? Isn't it just pure luck that causes one man to be delivered and his neighbor to be slaughtered?

Aha! You're asking Job's question.

Of all people Job was realistic about prayer. It was no magic cure-all for him. In fact, he refused to take the prescribed path—humility, humble submission—to salvation. For him prayer was struggling with God. It was not an attempt to escape from the harsh realities of life, but a wrestling match with the heart and soul of life itself. God was not a great cosmic problem-solver who exacted self-effacement as the price for his help. Not for Job!

There are always people around to explain our difficulties. They feel that they have life and its mysteries down pat. In Job's time it was people like his friends who insisted that everything that happens to us is judgment for our misdeeds or reward for piety and righteousness. Those who died in the foxholes, they would answer, deserved this punishment, while God was well-disposed to those who survived for some reason or another.

Today's Job

We have secular counterparts to Job's friends in our own day. When Archibald MacLeish adapted Job for a modern audience (in a play entitled *JB*), he had Job's friends spout the most recent philosophical and scientific theories to account for his suffering. Yes, we will always have people around with glib answers to impenetrable enigmas.

The basic problem with MacLeish's modern know-it-alls is that they were not religious. Hence, the real conflict between Job and his companions over the proper way to pray was lost. Interestingly, MacLeish's Job is not a man of prayer either, so the whole drama of prayer is replaced by a drama of learning from experience. MacLeish's is a very flat and empty world in which humans learn to live without a real God.

The real Job was a man of prayer and his drama was a drama of prayer. His dispute with his companions was over the proper way to pray. Job insisted upon praying in the "traditional" manner of the Psalms, and his companions stood up for a rational religion that was seeking to silence this type of prayer. They found Job's prayer insulting to God and tried to shut him up.

How Do We Pray?

To understand Job's prayer, we need to reflect for a moment on how we pray. Our prayer consists chiefly of *petition* or *supplication.* That is, we make requests; we ask God to do things for us. In personal prayer I may ask Him to deliver me from some threat to my life and well-being, from illness and death, from broken relationships and conflict, from job insecurity and failure. I may seek divine guidance in important decisions and actions. Oftentimes I appeal to God to give me courage, humility, a feeling of thanksgiving, or some other worthy attitude. Finally, I may pray for God's presence, forgiveness, and mercy, and relief from doubt and anxiety.

Petition was a significant part of both Old and New Testament prayer too. The individual worshiper sought deliverance from illness and death, hostilities and betrayal, economic and legal trouble, infertility and loss of family and friends. He or she, too, prayed for God's presence and forgiveness, and sought a stronger faith and hope.

There is one great difference between Old Testament prayer and our own. When a person experienced affliction and loss in those days, he or she would *accuse* God of betrayal and *cry out* for an explanation and would *complain* about the assault of his or her enemies and loss of friends and would tell God of his or her suffering and anguish. A person's utterances in prayer were like those we make to a friend or loved one during a quarrel.

Old Testament Prayers

In the Old Testament, accusing God and complaining about one's suffering were common in prayer. We learn this from the Psalms, which include many prayers of individuals that complain and accuse. For example, Psalm 22 begins with accusing questions:

My God, my God, why hast thou forsaken me?
Why art thou so far from helping me,
    from the words of my groaning?

God is accused of betrayal. Where is the salvation promised those who rely upon Him? He had been a saving help throughout life, but now He allows the supplicant to go under. Why doesn't He help when He is needed?

Psalm 22 is beloved by Christians because Jesus repeated the first accusing question as he was dying on the cross. Jesus felt kinship with the sufferers of the past and was not afraid to address God in their rugged words. These words have shocked many Christians because they don't seem to square with the image of Jesus as submitting without question or complaint to God's will. Anyway, if Jesus knew that he was going to be raised from the dead, why would he express such doubt about God's salvation? The truth is that Jesus experienced his loss of God as severely as any sufferer of his people. By saying these words, he demonstrated once-for-all that it was not rebellion to speak out from one's heart in a time of distress. He validated the prayer of protest as an appropriate way of coming before God.

Psalm 88 is probably the nearest prayer in the Psalms to the utterances of Job. The psalmist accuses God repeatedly and vehemently, so much so that one becomes uneasy. After describing his descent toward the grave, he blames God:

> Thou hast put me in the depths of the Pit,
> > in the regions dark and deep.
> Thy wrath lies heavy upon me,
> > and thou dost overwhelm me with all thy waves (vv. 6-7).

He has called upon God continually, but he receives no help:

> But I, O LORD, cry to thee;
> > in the morning my prayer comes before thee.
> O LORD, why dost thou cast me off?
> > Why dost thou hide thy face from me? (vv. 13-14)

Will God wait until he is dead before he acts (vv. 10-12)? Try saying this psalm as a prayer some time and you will begin to realize how desperate it is. Here is a prayer that pulls no punches. How similar to Job's this prayer sounds! Read Job 30:20-23.

Jeremiah's "confessions" also sound a great deal like Job. In these prayers, Jeremiah unburdens his feelings about the suffering he must undergo to be the Lord's spokesman. In one he accuses God of seducing and raping him:

> O LORD, thou hast deceived me and I was deceived;
> > thou art stronger than I, and thou hast prevailed (Jer 20:7).

In another he reproaches God for betraying him:

> Wilt thou be to me like a deceitful brook,
> > like waters that fail? (Jer. 15:18)

Job too charges God with assaulting him (for example, Job 19:7-9) and reproaches the Lord for betraying him (most poignantly in 10:9-13). Job and Jeremiah are certainly spiritual ken.

Prayer Unworthy of God

Why was such forceful, even outrageous, language used in biblical prayer? It seems utterly unworthy of God. Shouldn't a faithful person always think well of his Creator? Isn't it immature to blame God for one's troubles?

This is precisely the way Job's prayer struck his friends. They felt that accusing God was out-of-bounds. Instead of accusing him, you should confess that God is righteous and just in all His dealings.Anyway, you might arouse His anger, and then where would you be? So confess your sins and plead for mercy!

Of course, one might say that the friends were too hard-nosed. The reasons for our suffering are unknown, but it is certainly not God's will—at least not in many cases. Just leave the mystery and pray for help and strength. I'm sure that would be the advice of the average minister or layperson today. It's the interpretation of Job my students give.

But this seemingly innocuous soft-line advice is evasive. It is no honor to God to protect him from reality. A God who cannot hurt cannot save. If God is the sovereign ruler of the world, anything that happens must be his responsibility. For the men and women of the Old Testament, at any rate, God was the cause of suffering or at least the one who allowed it to happen.

When your child dies, or your marriage fails, or your house is struck down by a tornado, or your cattle die of a plague, or your country is invaded, you have experienced the *wrath* of God. God was expressing his anger toward you. Far from being a primitive belief, this was the natural and inevitable conclusion to draw from faith in a living God, the Creator and Ruler of the whole world.

I think that one can sympathize now with the gutsy prayer of Job, Jeremiah, the psalmists, and Jesus in his last agonizing hours. Whether God's anger was deserved or not, the one who suffered from it could not help but be angry and distraught. Old Testament prayer honestly expressed the feelings we all have. Going to God "cleared the air" and reestablished lines of communication.

What happened to make us lose this kind of prayer? Well, the religious thinking and sensitivity represented by Job's companions won the day, and the prayer of protest fell silent. In times of extreme distress, the urge to accuse God wells up in us still, for it is a very natural response. But we now feel that accusing God would be a lapse of faith. Only in the midst of the most unbearable events do we venture to lay it on the line. One hears, for example, of Jews who accused and even cursed God during their internment in Hitler's death camps. Who could do anything else?

Old Testament Prayer Was Honest

Old Testament prayer is a witness to us from an age when it was considered OK to say such harsh things. Prayer was honest and therefore real. Prayer was the conversation that told one's story, for life was confronted and shaped by honest dialogue with the Lord of life. The drama of life was made up of cries to God, and the meaning of life was to receive His answer.

We often use the phrase "God answers prayer." We mean by this that

God grants us what we request. What we ask for in our prayer comes to pass. As Lord of life He has the power to arrange events to meet our needs and free us from distress. If we do not receive what we asked for, either we feel let down or we conclude that God still acted for our good. We might even conclude that we did not know what was best for us when we prayed, and that God gave us what we really needed instead.

To say "answer" is somewhat strange if you really think about it. It suggests that God says something, that He enters into dialogue with us. To us this can only be a metaphor. God may act in response to our request, and thus touch us with His presence and concern. Hence, His action can be a communication to us, though not actual words.

The Old Testament man or woman hoped for actual words from God. Often when a person laid out his or her heart before God in the sanctuary a priest or prophet would communicate a word of God. He or she would be assured that the prayer had been heard and the request granted. I believe that we often come away from a prayer with a feeling of assurance. In the Old Testament era this assurance was articulated.

If prayer was the very heart of life, receiving a word from God was much more important than simply giving the supplicant assurance of deliverance. It re-established communication with one's life-partner. Prayer is the giving and receiving of words between us and the one who really matters, the Holy One whose attitude toward us makes all the difference in the world.

Job's Drama Ends with Reconciliation

The drama of Job ends when God speaks to him and turns his words of accusation and complaint into words of praise and rejoicing. This answer was Job's salvation. It was more important than anything else God might do. Just think what an odd and perverse ending the drama would have had if God had simply given him back children and twice his lost estate (Job 42:12-13). Job would have learned nothing. He would not know the meaning of God's act. Perhaps God was simply oiling the wheel that squeaks. Job certainly would not have encountered this awesome and yet loving God who addressed him from the whirlwind. What a difference the words make! God's word validated Job's integrity and his own righteousness and effected reconciliation.

I'm sure you're asking: How can we expect to hear actual words from God in response to our prayer? Isn't that only something that happens in the Bible? We don't have any priests or prophets around who communicate God's answer, unless it's the words of assurance after the prayer of confession (and many services don't have either of these anymore). We might be expected to pray like biblical people, but we can't be expected to receive God's answers.

The world's uncanny! Who knows what to expect? I didn't say that you are supposed to pray like the men and women of the Old Testament and I don't say that you should expect God's verbal answers. But who knows?

Prayer to be prayer must be honest and realistic. We must invest it with all of the significance of life itself, for it is the most important thing in our life or it is nothing. And to be realistic, we must pray in the expectation of an answer, in the hope that God will address us and let us know what He is about. Listen closely when you pray!

Daily Prayer Is Important

The kind of prayer that I have been describing belongs to the time of crisis, a time like Job experienced—which we will all experience in greater or lesser intensity sometime in our lives. But prayer is not only for times of crisis, and we should not model our daily prayers after the prayer for times of crisis. We must have a sense of rhythm and balance, a sense of when to say what.

Without daily prayer with its calm dealing with small everyday things we will not be ready to pray in the time of trouble. We will not be familiar with God's presence or free to pour out our feelings before him. I'm not advising against prayers in crisis—even if you've never prayed—but I am encouraging a daily routine of prayer. Prayer should set the tone of your daily life and prepare you for the moments of truth.

Remember, prayer—like meditation—is good for one's physical and mental health! In our pragmatic age, it could come with no higher recommendation. Try it, don't feel self-conscious! Get off by yourself and talk to your heart's content. It's good for you!

Don't wait until you believe that you have everything sorted out. So you doubt the very existence of God from time to time. So you doubt that He cares for you even if He does exist. So you doubt that He can do anything even if He is listening. These are precisely the questions to be hashed out with God in prayer.

Finally, I might warn you not to ignore repentance and humility. It would be a bad lesson to learn from Job that we can stride before God in good conscience. Job insisted upon his righteousness when he felt that he had been unfairly attacked by God. He was indeed a righteous man, more righteous than you or I will ever be. But even he would have been humble and penitent during good times. None of us is so righteous that before God's holiness we do not feel uneasy and even a bit cheap. Yes, at times we must stand up for our integrity, but true and passionate honesty must also puncture our self-conceit.

Rewards and Punishments

Not only do Job and his companions divide over the proper way to pray, they have quite a doctrinal dispute going. They disagree over the religious doctrine of rewards and punishments. According to this doctrine, God rewards people for their good behavior and faithfulness and punishes those who deviate from the way. Job's companions believe whole-heartedly in this doctrine, and Job is just as passionate in his rejection of it. Since this doctrine continues to attract adherents among Christians, I believe that it would be beneficial for us to delve into Job's refutations of the doctrine.

God Is Just and Righteous

Let's begin where the Bible begins: God is just and righteous. This is the common testimony of the Bible. Whenever a story is told in which God is a participant, He sets the standard for right and wrong. He cannot act immorally. It would be impossible for Him, say, to cheat, lie, or take pleasure in human suffering. We know from His commandments and laws that He doesn't approve of such things, and therefore it goes without saying that He would not violate His own will.

It's tempting to conclude that since God is just and righteous, whatever happens must be just and right. Isn't God the cause of every happening? When good times come, isn't it God who is to be thanked? When calamity and misfortune strike, isn't it God who ordains it? If God is just, as He must be, aren't good times a sign of His blessing? Bad times a sign of His punishment for wrong?

Does Divine Justice Prevail?

So much for theory—how about experience? Do good men and women reap the benefits of their deeds and evil, and godless persons suffer for their misdeeds? Job's companions Eliphaz, Bildad, and Zophar sincerely believed that observation, and experience confirmed the doctrine. Watch the fate of the wicked—they tell Job—and you will see that they always reap the harvest of their deeds. Such a person may succeed for a while. He may get by with exploiting and persecuting the righteous, but sooner or later his deeds come back to haunt him. His health fails in the prime of life, his house falls down, his land produces only weeds, his cattle die of plague—you name it. If he actually survives to old age, he will be forgotten in death or his children will suffer for the sins of their father.

Divine justice, they believed, never fails. The wicked may be allowed to rise to great heights, but only so that their fall will be all the more spectacular. As the old adage goes, "give him enough rope and he will hang himself."

This belief cannot be said to be old-fashioned and out-of-date. It seems to be a natural way of thinking. It is certainly very common among religious people around the world. The religions of India and China have full-blown versions of the same doctrine, and it seems to flow through the veins of Jews and Christians.

The Doctrine in Modern Life

In fact, the doctrine of rewards and punishments seems to be so natural that it's like an instinct. Children latch onto it before they learn anything else religious. Although my wife and I have never taught our pre-school age son that God will punish you if you're bad and reward you if you're good, he has recently begun expressing such beliefs. And when he hears that Santa Claus "knows when you've been bad or good," he has this doctrine driven home.

Not only young children think in these terms. Again and again I am amazed to find sophisticated people holding it. My college students tend to force every biblical teaching under it. Sin brings God's punishment, while faith and good works receive His reward. Even when a student has begun to doubt the truth of this belief, he is sure that the Bible teaches it. Religion, in the common mind, teaches rewards and punishments, and the Bible is the religious book to end all religious books.

Why is this doctrine so deeply embedded in our minds and hearts? Don't you think that we're sure that it has to be this way? We chastise our children for bad behavior, our society punishes criminals and other deviants, we hope that cheats and back-biters will suffer. On the other hand, those of outstanding moral character should be rewarded. If virtue isn't rewarded, wouldn't we do anything to gain advantage?

Wouldn't our society return to the jungle if we could do what we please and get away with it? Once a person or society begins to doubt that people receive what they deserve, the social order is in danger. Once you realize that being nice may make you come in last, it's not likely that you will continue to be nice. Once members of a society become cynical about serving each other, it becomes each one for himself. How fragile is the tissue that keeps us from devouring each other!

How fragile indeed when one faces the facts! For every example of just punishment for skulduggery that one can think of, one can also think of a scoundrel honored as a benefactor of mankind. When Job brings this to the attention of his companions, they have only the rather lame reply that the scoundrel's children will suffer for the sins of their father. Well, even that is doubtful—and it isn't very fair even if it were true. I think that we have to admit with Job that the doctrine of rewards and punishments doesn't fit our experience.

The innocent and righteous don't even receive the satisfaction of knowing that their works stand while the works of the wicked crumble. Many of the greatest contributions to human culture and civilization were made by ruthless, vain, arrogant, obnoxious people. All you have to do is think of the great conquerers—Alexander, Caesar, Napoleon—or the "captains of American industry." It seems as though selfishness and aggressiveness are the driving forces of human creativity. If there is any good in our creations, it must be due to God's power to turn evil into good.

Death Is the Great Leveler

Let us not forget the fact that death awaits us all. It levels all distinctions. Whether we have been upstanding or ruthless, we all end in the grave. Shouldn't we organize our lives to get the most out of the moment? "Eat, drink and be merry, for tomorrow we die." But death won't even let us escape into pleasure. Our time is always running out, the arrow cannot be halted in flight. As Job says so beautifully,

My days move more quicky than a weaver's shuttle
to reach my future's end (7:6).

The harsh facts of life have been brought home to Job by his sudden fall. He can no longer protect himself from them by wealth and security, moral integrity and good works. Now he knows the emptiness and vanity of all our striving, our loves, our good works.

You must remember that Job had no consolation when he confronted death. There was no hope of individual survival among Jews before or during the time when the book of Job was written. What happens in death is horrifying—

Straightway I will go and not return,
to a land of dark and shadow,
a night land, gloom, dead black,
black shining in black (10:21-22).

Death annihilates the individual personality. It means the loss of everything. All relationships are severed, all memory is lost, one's soul decays with one's body (14:21-22).

If we cannot expect earthly rewards and punishments and death erases all distinctions anyway, what difference does living a righteous and godly life make? I know what many of you would say—"There are rewards and punishments after death. Unlike Job, we Christians believe in a final judgment in which the score is settled." There is truth in this answer. Job himself moves toward a belief in an afterlife. But let's not speak too quickly about final judgment or shortcut the struggle Job went through.

When you believe in rewards and punishments after death, you have admitted that life here and now is not just. You give up any hope of supporting the doctrine of rewards and punishments with evidence from experience and base it solely on faith. Belief in a final judgment is belief in the justice of God despite the evidence, not because of it. We shall discover that it is like the belief that virtue is its own reward and vice its own punishment.

Job Is Still Committed to Righteousness

Back to Job. He had abandoned all belief in rewards and punishments in this life. The innocent and righteous suffer outrages and the wicked prosper, and God does nothing about it. But despite his despair over justice in life, he did not abandon hope in the justice of God. He continues to believe that righteousness and religious faith make a difference. His protest against God's unfairness is in the name of his own integrity. He won't go along with his friends and put on a show of repentance because truth and integrity are too important. Surely God wouldn't require us to lie in order to gain His favor!

86

The reward Job hoped for was simply of being approved by and reconciled with his God. When Job had his life fall apart on him, the worst part of it was his loss of God. God had become an enemy bent on his destruction. If Job could just renew his relationship with God, if God would just acknowledge his innocence and show a friendly face, that would be enough.

Between this hope and Job stood death. If he died too soon, he would not be reconciled with God. God might change His demeanor too late. But wait—Could God suspend the destructiveness of death until they had been reconciled? Perhaps death might be a "hiding place" for Job until God was ready to clear up his case.

If only You would hide me in the underworld,
conceal me there until Your wrath has passed,
and appoint a time to meet me (14:13).

But no sooner does he broach this possibility than he rejects it as impossible. How can a dead man be alive?

However, as he becomes more and more convinced that he can't hold out until God changes toward him, he begins to cling to the hope of reconciliation after death. In two very dramatic passages he utters the hope that his death itself might provoke an inquiry and out of the inquiry will come a vindication of his name. In the second of these he calls out:

O that my words were written down! . . .
For I am certain that my vindicator exists,
one who will someday testify on this spot (19:23-25).

His protests of innocence and accusations against God must be preserved to be used as evidence in a trial after his death. He will be represented by someone—a supernatural vindicator, perhaps God, perhaps another being—who will force God to admit that a mistake was made, that Job was not guilty and did not deserve the shoddy treatment that he got. Once this has been established, God will be reconciled with Job. Indeed, Job will experience it, will "see God on his side, . . . no longer alien and hostile" after he is dead! Impossible? Yes—but God can do the impossible. If He created man, He is capable of raising the dead to life! Or whatever it takes to rectify the injustices of life.

Christian's Have Confidence in God's Power

The Christian believes that Jesus was raised from the dead, and this gives us even more confidence in God's power to save the dead as well as the living. Jesus was like Job in suffering undeservedly. He was righteous, indeed the very image of what a person should be, yet he was hounded, persecuted, and finally crucified as a criminal, as an enemy of humanity and blasphemer of God. No greater injustice has ever occurred in human history. But death was not victorious, God showed that He could right wrong even when the victim was dead. He gave Jesus the justice that he had not gotten in life, and in doing so offered mercy to his persecutors.

We can no longer conceive of God without the power and intention of raising the dead and righting the wrongs that have occurred in this life. We realize that God must have power over death to be God, for He has demonstrated this power in raising Jesus from the dead.

But Job does not know these things and must struggle haltingly toward faith in God's power over death. To his people one must experience justice in this life or he will never experience it. Job must break through this hidden limitation placed upon the power of God to save. If God is truly in control and truly concerned about His creatures, He must not be impotent in the face of death. This Job discovers in his moment of desperation.

The Outcome of Job's Story

The outcome of Job's story, of course, is not the same as Jesus'. He receives a revelation and reconciliation with God in his lifetime, and even has what he lost returned to him. His hopes are fulfilled in this life so the hope expressed in a moment of desperation is never tested. For us who know this hope in Jesus Christ, however, we can see that Job was driven to a true and powerful understanding of God's ways.

When Job receives an answer from God, he has his hope fulfilled. He has his innocence confirmed, even his stubbornness has been rewarded. His story has a happy ending. Of course, he was corrected by God as well—but correction itself can work out for his good, and does.

God never explains to Job why he had to suffer, but He leaves no doubt about Job's innocence. Perhaps there are no answers to such questions as: Why do the innocent suffer? Why does God allow evil in His creation? But God can rectify the situation. He can clear the name of the innocent and overthrow the powers of evil.

God clearly denies that He is to blame when the innocent suffer (40:8). He is free from our human logic, having the power to define the situation simply by deciding that's the way it is. When He regards Job as innocent and yet denies blame, He speaks as a Judge who has the power to declare what's what. He is a just Judge simply by declaring the innocent innocent.

As for Job, he is rewarded after all. The kind of reward he receives cannot be mistaken with the kind of reward Job's companions believe in. It is not a payment for services rendered, it is not materialistic good fortune. No, Job's reward is spiritual: He is vindicated and reconciled with God. That is what mattered to Job, not the return of all that he had (How could he get his children back anyway?).

So the answer of the Book of Job to our desire for justice is that Job's story ends appropriately. The outcome is fitting to Job's struggle. God shows that He can pull it out of the fire. We all like stories with happy endings, and so does our God.

There is another lesson to learn from the story of Job. There is an old saying that goes: "Virtue is its own reward." There is a significant truth in this saying, and Job's vindication and reconciliation confirm this truth. We are the people we make ourselves to be, and our creation may be beautiful or ugly, noble or disgusting.

Job Benefits from His Righteousness

Job reaps the benefits of being a righteous person. Before he experienced God's revelation, his righteousness hardly seemed like an advantage. If he had sinned grievously, he would have had an explanation for his troubles and he would have known the prescription. The fact that his conscience was clear and that he had made honesty the stuff of his life made it impossible to accept his companions' prescription. He was too honest to lie, even if he thought it might bring God's favor. He was, as it were, stuck with his integrity.

Yet, it was an honor to be the man of integrity that he was. To be a person of such integrity that one is honored to be what he or she is, that is indeed a priceless reward. Imagine, a conscience that did not nag and grind away at one's self-respect! It took fortitude to insist on his integrity—Job too had to fight back a sense of worthlessness before the searching scrutiny of God. But Job succeeded—succeeded because his integrity and honesty was so great that he could take no other stand.

He was a man of such integrity that he stood up for the innocent against human and divine assault alike. God must show that He respects integrity before He can receive Job's praise. When he felt that God would kill him before they were reconciled, Job went so far as to express his belief that he had a counterpart in heaven, an advocate for innocent humanity who would even call God to task for arbitrary attacks. At first this seems outrageous and arrogant. Perhaps it is. Yet, don't we believe that Jesus is our advocate? Doesn't he stand up for the innocent as well as offer mercy to the guilty? Isn't this God Himself honoring integrity and righteousness?

If virtue is its own reward, vice is its own punishment. When we cheat, lie, and exploit, we become cheaters, liars and exploiters, and this is a terrible judgment to experience. We must live with the awful persons we are.

When one deforms his or her character, approach to God is cut off. A sinner cannot stand before the holy God. The holiness consumes him. This is when living with oneself becomes most intolerable. We may avoid facing up to what we are as long as we are by ourselves, but when we meet the God of righteousness we can only hide ourselves in shame and despair.

If Job had been unrighteous and idolatrous, as his friends had charged, he could not have stood to hear the words of God. They would have destroyed him. Job was over-awed by God, he was struck dumb, but he was not cut off. He had to yield his accusations, but he did not have to hide himself. God's presence was sweet and His words were comforting.

Let's return to the answer Job's companions Eliphaz, Bildad, and

Zophar gave to the question: Why should we be righteous and faithful? They believed it was quite practical. It pays off to conform to the law of life. There is no risk in being good, for it earns you God's favor. In other words, there are selfish reasons for being good—and that's not wise! What kind of goodness is it when it is motivated by selfishness? Isn't it a shallow and fake goodness that seeks rewards here on earth or rewards in heaven? Doesn't someone so motivated deserve—well, deserve themselves. They're not much better than the people they condemn.

In the prologue (chapters 1 and 2) the question was asked: Can any human serve God for unselfish reasons? Job is put through a trial to determine whether he has been honoring God for selfish or unselfish reasons, and he shows himself to be unselfish. The drama of Job (that is, chapters 3—42) presents us with a different Job, but still one who serves God for unselfish reasons. This Job holds fast to righteousness as the way of life for him. He knows that he will not be rewarded for his good deeds. He will live a righteous life because it is good and approved by God. When he receives God's revelation he discovers that he does receive a reward—the greatest of all, God's precious presence.

The God of the Whirlwind

Every story in the Bible is a story about God. The Bible was formed to present to believers the identity of their God—our God. It dramatizes for us how God thinks and feels, what He approves and disapproves of, what He has done, does and will do. It actually makes us intimately acquainted with the Creator of heaven and earth! We are taught to recognize God through the dramatic renderings of His character in Biblical prayers, stories, and prophecies.

In the Bible, God is working through our imagination to create an appropriate identity. We humans, as St. Paul says in Romans 1:23, are given to making idols resembling ourselves or even sub-human creatures. Our imaginations are not only weak, they are corrupted by our desire to have a God who meets our needs. The true God must judge and redeem what humans are saying about Him. He must create an identity in our minds that truly represents Him.

Job's is a story of God's redemption of human imagination. Job confesses at the end of the drama that before God's revelation he had only known God by what others had said about Him (42:5). Human language—the language of tradition, of orthodoxy, of Job's friends—had actually hidden the true God by creating a false and unsuitable portrait. God condemns the friends' misrepresentation (42:7). Job's own imagination, too, had gone a bit wild and God had to redeem his language too. However, God found something to build upon in what Job said, so he was commended for it (42:7).

The language of Job's companions closed off God's revelation, but Job's language prepared him to recognize the One who spoke to him from the whirlwind. When God spoke to him, He built upon what Job had said. He established His true identity by acting in character with the person Job imagined Him to be. He changed Job's image of Him by identifying with it and redeeming it from within.

Remember, God seems to be a hostile tyrant to Job. Job had formed an image of God's character from the teachings of his people and his personal experiences. Before this great crisis, his image had been satisfying and sweet. God seemed to help him in every undertaking. The common beliefs of his people suited him well. But the crisis changed all of that. The doctrines expressed by his companions now seemed false, and the God they believed in had become Job's enemy, a Judge who had passed sentence upon him without specifying the charges but who demanded Job's confession of guilt. The God he had known had turned sour.

To appreciate Job's situation, perhaps a contemporary example will help. The Russian prisoners whose stories are told in Solzhenitsyn's *Gulag Archipelago* (Harper & Row, 1974) had been believers in Marxism. Then they had been condemned by the higher authorities without a trial or any honest explanation. Someone somewhere had decided that they should be singled out as enemies of the people, and it made little difference whether they had committed illegal acts. To add to the perversity of the situation, the authorities demanded confessions of guilt from the prisoners to break their wills and make a show of justice. All you have to do is substitute "God" for "higher authorities" and you have Job's situation.

God's Action Demonstrates His Love

Now, what is God going to do to redeem His good name and deliver Job from his bitterness? He has little freedom to maneuver. He must meet the God of Job's imagination head-on. This image is not a false God, as the friends' is, but the true God forcing Job out of the dogmas of his people toward a truly just and saving God. The hostile tyrant of Job's imagination must be redeemed, not shattered.

God turns the story around simply by entering it. Simply by breaking His silence He demonstrates to Job that He is not alien and hostile. He comes to Job in his distress and thereby exhibits His justice and love for His creature. He establishes justice by answering the prayer of a righteous man. He demonstrates His love by seeking Job's welfare.

Of course, God could have spoken so harshly that He simply reinforced Job's image of Him as a tyrant. Eliphaz, Bildad, and Zophar wanted Him to. They would have Him put Job in his place. He should learn that he deserves whatever he suffered and more (cf. 11:5-6). Their religion demanded humility and submissiveness of men and women before God, so Job's defiance and independence must be punished.

God Remains Aloof

But God had an entirely different problem. He could not act like a tyrant, for a tyrant does not deserve the respect of his subjects. The Lord of the world must show that He is worthy of praise. Only by doing so can He set up His throne in the hearts of the righteous. How can God be God and a righteous man or woman go to perdition for his or her integrity? Most people would knuckle under simply because God has the power of life and death, but God wants to win those who possess the integrity and courage not to knuckle under.

No sooner is this said, though, than we court a misunderstanding. When God meets with a person, He insists on being God. We modern American Christians might expect God to try to win Job over with kindness, to comfort him with expressions of sympathy, to curry his favor like a presidential candidate does the voters. No, God is not running for office, and He doesn't want to be a "buddy." The God who speaks to Job is positively standoffish. He keeps His distance. We get no glimpse into His thoughts or feelings. And He doesn't so much as mention Job's name, let alone pat him on the back.

God isn't always so standoffish in the Bible, but Job needs it. He has expressed the hope of meeting God as an equal. He has accused God as if he were a moral superior to his Creator. He expects God to meet his standards or else. Against such impertinence, God can only force Job to recognize the infinite abyss that separates them.

God Censures Job

Look at God's censures of Job. At the outset He charges him with muddling the discussion (38:2), and at the beginning of the second address he is reprimanded for "condemning me to prove your innocence" (40:8). Job is being forced to recognize the gulf between them. Job does not possess the knowledge, power, and grace of a god, so he cannot presume to accuse the One who does. Likewise, since Job is only a man he cannot judge God to be unjust though he has suffered undeserved punishment. Human beings simply can't make any accusation against God stand, for God determines what is right and just. Job's accusations were not out-of-bounds (God can certainly tolerate critics of His regime!), but they are not the last word. At the appropriate moment it becomes necessary to abandon the charges—because they don't stand up, they lose their force once God answers.

God's interrogation of Job also establishes the gulf between them, but it leads in a more positive direction as well. The questions force Job to admit that he is a creature and also that God deserves praise as Creator and Redeemer. Every question has the answer "not I, but God." Of course I don't know how the foundations were suspended in the void, but God does. Of course I don't have the power to command the clouds, but God does. Of course I cannot trample kings and nations under foot, but God can. All these questions lead away from Job and his problems to the praise of God.

In all of these questions God returns to things Job and his companions had already mentioned. Bildad had, for example, repeated a psalm praising the Creator's great power and wisdom (26:5-14). He ends rather marvelously:

We get only an inkling of what He does.
Who can imagine the full thunder of His power (26:14)?

This praise is quite worthy of God, but Bildad and his friends misuse it. They think: If God is this powerful and wise, how imperfect and insignificant man must be in His eyes (25:4-6). If he is this powerful and wise, how can anyone doubt that whatever happens is just?

Job, too, praises God the Creator, and his praise is distorted. In answer to Bildad, he agrees that God is supreme in power and wisdom, but this makes Him terrifying (9:2-13). God's power is destructive, dark, and leaves man helpless:

When He decides to rob and kidnap,
            who can dissuade him? (9:12)

Job also praises God for creating him personally, but again he turns the praise into accusation:

Your own hand formed and shaped me,
and now You turn around and destroy me. . . .
I know You planned this from the beginning (10:8, 13)

So Job is not a disbeliever, he acknowledges God in traditional language, but he cannot praise God; he can only brood over this sinister being.

When God interrogates Job, He quotes him against himself. You, Job, have admitted that I have this power and wisdom, that I am Creator and Provider—now, can you still say these things in the accusing tone that you did before? Don't you have to admit that it's really some wisdom and power that I have? Don't you have to admit that I've really pulled off some great ones? Do you really think my creations are botched? Come on, see if you can accuse me now?

God Describes the World He Created

God has another weapon up His sleeve that Job wasn't prepared for—exquisite poetry. These are words truly worthy of God. The erection of the world takes shape before our eyes; the dawn breaks and the world takes on the spectrum of the rainbow; we imagine ourselves visiting heavenly storehouses to inspect the rain, sleet, snow, and wind. Remember how God adds delightful detail? The heavenly choir sings at the laying of the foundations. God takes delight in watering the wasteland because it is useless to man. Little birds cry to God; the horse snorts and charges into battle; the eagle scans the horizon from the edge of a cliff. What a glorious God to have created a world pulsing with such beauty!

Every act of creation and providence is described in very human terms. Why? Because Job is being asked whether he is the creator. If Job were to make a world, he would erect it like a building. If he were to subdue the primeval waters, he would dam them like a river. If he were to control the weather, he would store the rain, hail, snow, and wind in storehouses and truck them out at the appropriate time. The metaphors are not to be taken as descriptive of God's actions, but of the way we humans would have to do it if we were in God's place. Job is made to contemplate his puny building programs, then look up at the infinite heavens and think about building them. A carpenter friend of mine once put this thought beautifully: "Here, I can't even saw a straight cut, so think of what a carpenter it took to make this universe."

The metaphorical, rhapsodic description of creation protects our language from being taken too literally. No human description can really describe how God created the world. But we are often tempted to think that it does. We often are tempted to take the creation account in Genesis 1 as an explanation of the origin of the universe. We are tempted to treat it, say, as an alternative to evolutionary theory. Genesis 1 tempts us to take it literally precisely because it is without images or poetry, though it is beautiful and solemn. It has the appearance of a straightforward scientific account, though in reality, it is not. Job 38-39, on the other hand, is so poetic and imaginative that we realize immediately that God's creative acts are beyond human comprehension. All we can do is contemplate our piddly little creations, then think how much more wisdom, power, and grace it took to create a universe. Our creation language really points to the mystery of God and the amazing fact that there is a world at all. Job 38-39 teaches us the way to read all our attempts to imagine creation.

Other Poetic Descriptions

The poet of Job is not alone in describing creation in highly poetic terms. The prophet known as Second Isaiah describes the Creator's grandeur and power in moving, transporting language (Isaiah 40:12-26).

He sought to give his people courage and hope in the midst of the despair of the Babylonian exile. Creation is supreme evidence of His power. The poet of Job also seeks to convince Job of God's saving power, but to do so he must first convince him that God is worthy of praise—a glorious, sublime, fantastic Creator.

Job 39 is devoted to God's creation and care of the animals. This theme unites it with Psalm 104, which also celebrates God's wondrous providence. All living beings rely upon God for breath, food, water—all things necessary for life. Here we have almost romantic poetry, with God as the life-force animating the teeming world of nature.

We Must Know God Himself

But hold it! Let's not get carried away with nature worship. Nature is sub-personal, so God cannot meet us there in His true personal identity. Nature reveals Him as an artwork reveals the artist. We sense the mind and heart of the artist; we receive a communication from him. Likewise, the heavens and the earth, the forces of nature, and living creatures all tell us of their Creator. But we cannot speak to the artist when we know him only through his artwork, and we cannot serve God when we know Him only through His creation. He must enter our stories; He must meet us personally and interact with us if we are to get to know His character.

So God's second address turns away from nature to human affairs, where He makes Himself known as a Person. Again Job and his companions had described God as the ruler of human history, so God has language to build upon. Eliphaz had praised God for raising up the powerless and overthrowing the crafty (5:8-16). The true God is worshiped in these words. However, Eliphaz and his friends are convinced that God so rules our lives that our stories are all melodramas. The good always win; the wicked always lose. Job comes back with a tragic account of human affairs (12:7-25). All the dreams and efforts of men and women are destined to destruction. All persons of position and honor are overthrown to show that only God is on top. Is God envious of human success?

What can God say to turn Job's language around? How can He show Job that He isn't malicious? How can He show Job that He does not laugh at the trials of those who depend upon Him? He certainly cannot re-assert the friends' doctrines! But then, how can He escape the judgment that He is not just and loving or He is not in control? How can He be both good and powerful?

God Challenges Job

Well, God challenges Job to take up the task of overthrowing the mighty and powerful (40:9-14). If he could do that, he could save himself. The irony of human history is that we have continually tried to do just that—we have tried to control our own destiny; we have tried to save ourselves, but we cannot. Throughout the Bible our power to save ourselves is denied and our attempt to do so condemned as the height of sin. Because humans do attempt to save themselves, God must overrule them. Take the affirmation of Psalm 33:10-11:

The LORD brings the counsel of the nations to nought;
He frustrates the plans of the peoples.
The counsel of the LORD stands for ever,
the thoughts of His heart to all generations.

God alone can save because He alone can achieve His purposes and determine the outcome of ours.

Job—God says—you must decide whether you are going to try to save yourself and put yourself at odds with Me, or rely on Me for salvation. Job's questioning of God's justice and benevolence is turned upside down: Is Job going to seek to save himself, thereby joining God's enemies, or is he going to acknowledge that he is a creature who must receive salvation from God's hand?

With a rather surprising and ironic twist, God concludes by challenging Job to take on Leviathan. Job had asked God in his very first prayer (7:12) why God was treating him as if he were the sea monster (using another name, Tannin). Now God points out how impotent Job is by recalling the same monster. Job has been challenging God, yet he can't even stand up to one of God's creatures. How could Job have expected to win his case against God? Did he realize what he was getting into? Doesn't he know that whenever God enters into a struggle with a creature, the creature is helpless?

Doesn't God sound unfair? Isn't He avoiding Job's questions by attacking his right to ask them? Isn't He pulling rank on Job? Isn't He requiring blind obedience from Job?

God Is the Supreme Judge

If God were a finite creature, such questions would be to the point. If He were a creature, it would be wrong to count all of His opponents enemies of right and truth. If He were a creature, He would have to submit to a higher court of judgment. But the Creator is the final court; He is the One who establishes what is right and true. And what is right and true must always win or the universe would be in an awful state.

We need not join Job's companions to acknowledge the righteous and powerful God. Their opinion is not the common opinion of biblical writers. The vast majority realize that there is evil and injustice in God's world, yet believe God to rule it justly. The evil that arises out of our rebellious hearts, and even the evil in nature itself, forms the background to all of God's actions. The grip of evil on us is the main theme of the Bible, not a fact that has been swept under a rug.

According to the Bible, there is a pitched battle going on between the powers of this world and God for control. In this struggle the innocent and righteous suffer outrages, for the forces of retribution operate slowly and indirectly. God fights fire with fire. He uses evil and selfish people to punish evil and selfish people; He uses victims of injustice to arouse the consciences of avengers; He uses the forces of injustice and falsehood to keep the forces of justice honest and realistic.

If there is a pitched battle between God and His creatures, and the results of the battle are often tragic, how can we believe in God's power to save? The testimony of the Bible is that though humans resist His will and create havoc, God always comes out the victor. Whenever He acts, He achieves what He sets out to do. Job's story is itself an example of the way God turns defeat into victory and injustice into justice and falsehood into truth. Job's undeserved suffering redeemed human imagination and established the identity of the true God.

Saved by God's Power and Justice

What is so amazing is that Job discovers that he is saved by the very power of God that seemed to make him a tyrant. No, he can't challenge God successfully—but that is now his source of hope. His defeat has turned into victory. God has overwhelmed him—and convinced him.

God does not have to silence His critics to establish His power and justice, for anything He does is completely effective and right and good altogether. He is quite free to acknowledge Job's innocence, for He doesn't have to establish His own righteousness at the expense of His creatures. He doesn't have to be defensive about His position; He can be completely self-assured. Whatever He does is right, whatever He does achieves His purpose. Since He cannot lose He does not have to win at the expense of His creatures.

Job has undergone an experience like Jacob's when he wrestled with an angel all night (Genesis 32:22-32). Jacob fought his opponent to a draw and even forced a blessing from him. At daybreak, when he realized that he had really been wrestling with God Himself, he had to confess that he was lucky to come out alive. One cannot wrestle with God and survive, let alone force a blessing from Him—unless God grants it. It is God who saves, He alone out of the bountifulness of His mercy.

Job could not challenge God and survive, let alone with approval—unless God grants it. God has indeed granted it, though, for in Job's victory God wins. He has won over Job to praise. He has not forced Job to abandon his integrity; He has convinced him that He is worthy of his creatures' praise. Glory be to God!

Appendix

This appendix is devoted to explanations of cuts, re-arrangements, and deviant translations to be found in the text of Job presented above. Since the book was written for non-scholars, it was felt that these somewhat technical matters should be put in an unobtrusive place. First I shall treat the major cuts and re-arrangements, and then offer comments on the verses that need explanation.

In chapter 32 another friend appears in the drama of Job, named Elihu. The majority of scholars believe that he is not original to the drama. He is not mentioned as present until he speaks, and he disappears without notice after he finishes. He does not speak when the others do. He speaks only one long diatribe (chapters 32-37). The speech comes at an awkward place, after the friends and Job have finished. Indeed, Elihu interrupts the natural connection between Job's challenge to God (chapter 31) and God's reply (chapters 38-41). Finally, Elihu does not really improve upon the discredited doctrines of the three spokesmen for orthodox religion. Elihu's speech was probably composed and inserted by a reader who was offended by our poet's devastating presentation of orthodoxy and sought to re-establish it. In any case, I have left Elihu's diatribe out of the drama.

I have made some other major cuts and re-arrangements. In most of these I followed the suggestions of Claus Westermann. You can find his reconstructions and reasoning in his book, *Das Aufbau des Buches Hiob*. In the following paragraphs I can give you a brief, simplified version of his thinking.

For some unknown reason, chapters 24-28 are all mixed up. First, there are not enough speeches here to fill out the third round of dialogue. A round consists of an address by each of the three friends and a response of Job to each. The first (chapters 4-14) and second (15-21) rounds are intact, and the third begins alright (22-23). But then there is chaos. Only one friend gets to speak (chapter 25:1-6), and his speech is much too short. Moreover, Job says things that are appropriate to his companions, not Job himself (26:5-14, 27:7-23). The confusion is compounded by passages that don't belong appropriately to anyone (probably 24:13-17, certainly 28:1-28).

There are good reasons for believing that chapters 24-27 are fragments that have been displaced from earlier parts of the drama and that chapter 28 is an independent poem. When Eliphaz, the lead-speaker in each round, delivers his third address (chapter 22), he condemns Job as evil and godless. This effectively cuts off communication between Job and his companions, so a continuation of speeches is dramatically anticlimactic and out-of-character. The more satisfying arrangement would be for Job to turn away from his friends and close off the dialogue. If we insert 27:5-6 before 23:3-17, we have the desired conclusion.

Portions of chapter 24 fit well with Job's one and only refutation of his companions' warnings that the wicked and godless always receive their due punishment (chapter 22). This is how we have treated it in the translation.

Chapters 25 and 26 fit well between chapters 8 and 9. Job in chapter 9:2 refers to an idea (no one is righteous before God) in the previous speech which is not to be found in chapter 8, but is expressed in 25:4-6. It has long been recognized that 25:2-3 belong with 26:5-14. Putting together these observations, we have re-arranged chapters 25-26 (25:2-3, 26:5-24, 25:4-6, 26:1-4) and inserted them between chapters 8 and 9.

Finally, we have inserted the portions of chapter 27 appropriate to one of the friends into chapter 11 (Zophar's speech). Chapter 11 lacks a description of how the wicked fall, and chapter 27 supplies it.

Chapter 28 is a special case. It doesn't suit either Job or his friends. Stylistically it doesn't seem to be by the poet who composed the drama. However, it provides a lovely comment on the drama, so I have preserved it (with 27:11-12 as an introduction) as an interlude spoken by a narrator (whose job it is to read the prologue and epilogue).

The addresses of God contain some puzzling portions, in particular the descriptions of the Ostrich (39:13-18), Behomoth, a hippopotamus (40:15-24), and Leviathan, a crocodile (41:12-34). Unlike the other descriptions of animals, these do not challenge Job to exhibit the power and intelligence of God. Only a portion of the Leviathan passage (41:1-11) does this. Interestingly, Leviathan is a mythological monster in these verses, but not in 41:12-34. This allows the second address to end on a dramatically appropriate note.

The following pages are devoted to comments on words in the text. The chapter and verse are given in the left-hand margin; the word or phrase in the text that I want to comment on is italicized, and the comments follow the colon. When I deviated from the literal meaning of the Hebrew but felt that no defense of my rendering was needed (or perhaps was possible!), I simply give the literal translation without comment. I feel that I should acknowledge my deviations, doing homage to objective reality. When I followed an emendation suggested by the critical apparatus in *Biblica Hebraica*, ed. by Kittel, 7th Ed. (the Hebrew text I translated from), I simply say "emended to yield this sense," or something to that effect. When I followed a specific commentator, I give him credit by name. My other remarks should be self-explanatory.

TRANSLATION NOTES

1:1   *Uz:* The identity of this country or region is uncertain.

  6   *The day.* . . . New Year's Day, when according to Israel's neighbors the gods assembled for a great banquet and the "fates" were decided for the coming year. Only here in the whole Old Testament do we meet this polytheistic idea.

      sons of God: The name in the Old Testament for the divine beings subordinate to God. They were demoted to "angels" at the end of the Old Testament era.

      the Devil's Advocate: literally, "the Satan," the name later used synonymously with the Devil. To use Satan here is misleading, so I chose a title descriptive of his function in Job 1-2.

2:11   *Teman:* a region within Edom.

      Shuh: a region in Deom or Arabia, exact location uncertain.

      Naamah: location uncertain.

3:3   *The night when they shouted "A boy!":* lit. "the night said 'A man is conceived!' " This idea is rather farfetched, so I have followed a common modification.

  4,6   *I would have:* I have added these words to break the monotony of the series of "let's" and to indicate that Job is simply wishing that his day/night of birth would be punished for allowing him to be born.

8 *spell-binders and wierd magicians:* lit. "curses of the sea" and
   "those skilled in binding Leviathan (by magic)."

14 *ruins:* I take this to be ironic: The great building projects of rulers
    are vanity.

17 *In Sheol:* I have named the place referred to by "there" in the
    Hebrew.

4:10-11   *Lion . . . panther . . . young lion . . . leopard . . . lion-whelps:*
    The Hebrew terms all designate lions, but I have varied the species
    to break the monotony.

19 *creatures of mud houses:* Eliphaz may be speaking literally or
    metaphorically of the human body.
    "They are destroyed before a moth" has been deleted as unfitting.

20 *without notice:* reading "without a name" for the difficult
    "without setting."

21 *vaunted dignity:* The word could mean "tent cord" and be read as
    a metaphor for bodily existence.

5:5 *taken over by thorns and thistles:* lit., "and to from thorns he takes
     it, and he pants for (or snares) thirsty ones their wealth." Clearly
     the Hebrew is corrupt, and I have simply guessed at what it
     means.

7 *a man gives birth:* I have changed the vowels of the Hebrew to
   yield this reading,

9 *marvels and wonders:* translating the same word twice for poetic
   effect.

6:4 *God of war:* lit., simply "the Almighty." I have made the idea
     more explicit.
     He readies His torture-chambers for me: lit., "the terrors of God
     are drawn up against me."

10 *its finality:* lit., "pain which does not spare." I am guessing that he
    means the "final agony" of death.
    and put an end to myself: This has been added to identify the
    divine law that Job has in mind, *viz.,* the prohibition against
    suicide.

14 *friends:* I have made this plural to distinguish pronouns in the sec-
    ond line and connect the reference to Job's three friends.
    turned sour on religion: lit., "renounced fear of the Almighty."

15 *a creek:* From plural in Hebrew to singular in English.

25 *What harm:* lit., "What honest words are violent?"

7:5 *my scabs dry, my skin hardens, cracks and runs:* I have made the
     description more vivid than the Hebrew for effect.

7 *Remember, Lord:* The Hebrew lacks "Lord," it simply shifts to a
   second person singular pronoun indicating that Job is not talking
   to his companions or himself, but to God.

15 *(but) I loathe death more than suffering:* I have emended the text
    ("suffering" for "bones") and included the first word of the next

verse ("loathe") and added "but." I must admit that I am alone in my understanding of Job as saying that he fears death so much that he has not committed suicide to escape his suffering.

8:10 *Profound:* adding this word to explicate the meaning.

25:2-3, 26:5-14, 25:4-6. These verses have been moved here from the third round of speeches and arranged in a logical order (see above). Verses 25:2-3 belong with 26:5-14 as praise of the majesty of the creator. Verses 25:4-6 fits better *after* this praise than in the middle of it. The nothingness of man comes to mind when one contemplates the majesty of God. It must be admitted that this inserted portion of the speech (25:2-3, 26:5-14, 25:4-6) does not follow very smoothly on 8:20-22, indicating perhaps that a transition has been lost.

26:1-4 These verses have been moved here along with the block of material in Bildad's speech. They fill a need for some introductory address responding to the previous speaker before Job launches off into the body of his speech. Job's remarks are ironic and sarcastic in the extreme.

26:2 *all-powerless One:* lit., "(one) of no strength." I take him to be speaking of God, so I made it more explicit and heightened the sarcasm.
   3 *Since He doesn't know enough you have decided to advise Him:* lit., "How you have instructed one of no wisdom."
   4 *wise words:* adding "wise" to the text to heighten the sarcasm.

9:12 *dissuade Him:* lit., "turn Him back."
   14 *argue with Him:* lit., "answer Him."
   15 *refute Him:* lit., "answer Him."
   21 *I accept the risk:* lit., "I do not know my soul," i.e., have no regard for myself and therefore I am willing to risk myself in the name of my innocence. Job believes that insisting on his innocence might provoke God's wrath.
   22 *What difference does it make?:* lit., "It is the same. Therefore I say:"
   24 *forces of evil:* lit., "hand of the evil."
      eyes of justice: lit., "faces of its judges."
   28 *I tense up anticipating the next blow:* lit., "I fear all my wounds," which fits most smoothly into the context if it is interpreted to mean the wounds that are yet to come.
   32 *an equal:* lit., "like me."
      bring Him to task: lit., "I could answer Him."
   35 *for I am not anxious about myself:* lit., "for not thus (am) I with myself," the sense of which is not at all clear.

10:3 The verse continues: "and upon the plans of the wicked You shine." I have deleted it as out-of-mood with the highly personal language of the section.

104

9 *Remember, Lord:* adding "Lord."

12 *loyal and loving:* emending "living" to "loving."

21-22 *a land of dark and shadow,* etc.: I have not followed the Hebrew word for word.

11:9 *Doesn't He stretch:* added to make a complete sentence.

12 Deleted because it does not fit the context and its meaning is obscure.

27:13-23, 8-10. Moved here from the third round of speeches where it is inappropriately in Job's mouth. It fills the need in our speech for a description of the fate of the wicked to counterbalance the encouragement of Job to humble himself before God in the hope of being shown favor (11:13-20). Verse 27:13 is clearly an introduction, and 27:8-10 make a fitting conclusion, so we have rearranged the sections.

19 *He lies down . . . opens his eyes,* etc.: the end of the first line, "and he is not gathered (to his fathers in death)," has been deleted as without meaning.

8 *What hope is there for an irreverent man?:* Deleting "when he is cut off" as redundant.

10 *enjoy divine favor:* lit., "delight in the Almighty."
Will God meet him every time?: This is commonly read: "Will he call (to) God at all times?" but "God" can be construed as the subject of the verb and the godless man the object. God is supposed to come to the aid of the righteous man every time he calls, but God does not aid the godless.

11-12 There is no satisfactory place for these verses.

11:13 *toward God:* supplying "God" for "Him."

15 *a solid foundation:* lit., "you will be firmly established and not fear."

16 *leave your suffering behind:* lit., "forget trouble."

12:4-6: These verses break the train of thought between verses 3 and 7, so I have deleted them.

11-12: These verses break the train of thought between verses 10 and 13, so I have deleted them.

18 *lets loose judgment:* lit., "punishment of kings he lets loose."

21 *lords:* emending the nonsensical "water channels."

25 *invisible darkness:* lit., "they grope in darkness and no light." My rendering is a bit of a pun, meaning "darkness without visibility" and "darkness of a non-physical kind."

13:3 *for I . . . :* Replacing a simple conjunction to stress Job's desire to argue with God, not with his companions.

8 *unbalance the scales of justice:* lit., "lift up the face," a Hebrew idiom meaning "show partiality."

10 *arraign and condemn:* translating the same word twice according to its dual act/result meaning.

11 *Won't His majesty seize you with terror?:* lit., "Won't His fear overwhelm you?"
when you stand before Him: added to strengthen the image of a courtroom confrontation.

15 *and I expect Him to—:* lit., "I do not hope," which I have simply stated positively. Traditionally the text has been emended to yield the opposite meaning: "Though he slay me, yet will I hope in (or trust) Him."
argue my case: lit., "defend my ways."

17 *Let them ring in your ears:* lit., "My declarations (be) in your ears."

20 *But, Lord, . . . :* "Lord" added to signal the shift of addressees.

13:21 *don't overpower me with Your deity:* lit., "Do not terrify me (with) fear of you." Here and in verse 11 I have taken "fear" to be the numinous dread God causes in His creatures simply by His presence.

23 *What great evil am I guilty of?:* lit., "How great (or many) are my iniquities and sins?"
Expose . . . before my eyes: lit., "cause me to know."

24 *Why, why:* doubled for poignancy.

26 *branded:* lit., "cause to inhabit."

27 *and pegged my soles to the ground and then watched how I ran:* I have reversed the lines and drawn out the images.

28 Moved forward two verses where it fits fairly well in the description of man's dismal lot on earth.

14:4 Deleted as out-of-context and distracting.

14:12 *Never again . . . under heaven:* lit., "not until the heavens does he stir."

13 *to meet me:* lit., "to remember me," but the thrust of the thought is stronger than mere memory.

14 *O that I might endure:* I have supplied the words suggesting that he is expressing a wish. I would take the beginning of verse 13 as carrying over to verses 14, 15. The Hebrew could be translated "All the days of my warfare I would (or will) endure until relief comes." Against this, I do not believe that Job is contemplating reconciliation after death at this point. He has abandoned that hope (temporarily) in verse 14a.

15 *Lord, if only You would call:* Supplying "Lord" and the words suggesting that he expresses a wish. One could translate: "You will call and I . . . "

15:2 *Would one who is truly wise, etc.:* lit., "Would a wise man answer (with) windy knowledge and fill his belly (with) east wind?" I simply wanted to improve on Eliphaz's eloquence.

15:5 *twisted heart:* lit., "your iniquity. . . ."

9 *Does your mind,* etc: lit., "What do you perceive and it is not with us too?"

10 *Both age and experience:* lit., "Both the gray-haired and aged are with us."
our combined age: lit., "greater than your father's (are our) days."

11 *Does His word move too slow for you?:* Supplying "His" and emending slightly.

12 *Why do you let your passions master your mind?:* lit., "What has taken (away) your mind?"

13 *your ire:* following Marvin H. Pope's, *Job: Introduction, Translation, and Notes* (Anchor Bible, Vol. 15. Doubleday, 1965), pp. 106, 110.

14 *What in human nature is worthy of purity?:* lit., "What is man that he should be pure?"
creature born like an animal: lit., "born of woman," the meaning of which seems to be approximately what I said.

18 *well-known to the ancients:* Emending slightly to yield this sense.

19 Deleted as out-of-context.

22 *the sword lurks there for him:* lit., "he is spied out to the sword."

26 *He charges about shielded:* Shortening a rather bizarre image.

29 *he will not plant an enduring estate:* An impressionistic reading.

31 Deleted as out-of-context.

33 *a grapevine stripped of its clusters:* following Pope, *Job,* pp. 108, 113.

34 *irreligious man:* There is a set of Hebrew words meaning approximately the same thing: impious, wicked, unjust, etc., and I have not been translating any word consistently, but using whatever word that strikes my fancy.

16:2 *this before:* lit., "many such things."
Some comforters: lit., "miserable comforters."

3 *verbal abyss:* lit., "windy words."

4 *ringing phrases:* lit., "words."

6 *It's no use speaking,* etc.: lit., "If I speak, my pain doesn't subside. But (if) I cease, what would go away from me?"

7 *when I am down:* Supplied to evoke the particular thrust of this complaint.
to witness against me: lit., "for a witness it is."
incriminating evidence: lit., "My leanness arises against me, it answers to my face." I take my wording to be the sense of these awkward statements.

9c-11 Deleted because they break the train of thought: in verses 7-9b, God is the enemy, and he is again in verses 12-14. But in verses 9c-11 we have a group of human enemies.

12 *quietly, relaxed, unsuspecting:* translating the same word three times for effect.
jerked and twisted: translating the same word twice for effect.

13 *took careful aim:* lit., "surround me," a rather drab statement.

and struck my gut: reading this line as a continuation of the archery image.

without a miss: lit., "without pity."

17 *proven guilty:* lit., "no violence is in my hands." Job is asserting his innocence, and my rendering makes that more immediately apparent.

20 *I have poured out tears to God to find a friend for me:* A notoriously difficult verse. I have reversed the sequence of lines for simplicity and made the first a phrase designating what Job has · requested.

to find: emending the word which means either "mocker" or "interpreter."

a friend for me: reading as a singular.

17:3 *Please, Lord, deposit my pledge, etc.:* This verse is not at home in its context, so I have put it here, where it fits a bit better.

Lord: Supplied to signal address to God.

take the risk of vouching for me: lit., "shake my hand," a Hebrew idiom used to vouch for a person for a loan or in court.

16:22 *my numbered years:* Supplying "my."

to a close: Supplied to yield the sense I think is intended.

17:4a *You've made them stupid:* lit., "You have hidden their minds from insight."

4b-5: Deleted as out-of-context.

6 *You've:* emending the text from 3rd to 2nd person.

8-10: Deleted as out-of-context and disruptive of the train of thought between verses 7 and 11.

12 *Night becomes day:* lit., "They make night into day," perhaps with his companions as subject, but Job is not otherwise speaking about them here. Hence I took it impersonally.

light mingles with darkness: lit., "light draws near before the face of darkness."

16 *with me:* emended to yield this sense.

18:3 *dumb animals:* lit., "(Why) are we dumb in your eyes?"

4 *You tear your guts to pieces in rage:* The Hebrew is in third person and has a participle rather than a finite verb, yielding: "One who tears his soul in his rage."

guts: lit., "soul."

6 *room:* lit., "tent."

11 *he feels a pursuer:* lit., "they chase him at his heel."

12 *His power and wealth:* Translating one Hebrew word twice.

13 *Disease eats:* emended to yield this sense.

a killing ailment: lit., "the first-born of death," perhaps a disease thought to be the offspring of the god of death.

14 *king of terrors:* Alluding to the god of death, Mot, known to us now from Ugaritic literature.

15 *fire:* emended to yield this sense, following Pope, *Job,* pp. 124, 126.
18 *His compatriots:* Supplying a subject for "they" in Hebrew.
20 *his fate . . . the lesson his end teaches:* Supplied on the basis of the context. The Hebrew has only "at his day."
21 *living conditions:* lit., "the dwellings," a metaphor for the conditions of a person's life.
   sanctuary: lit., "place," a word often used for a holy place.

19:4 *my lament has broken bounds:* lit., "I have wandered astray," probably in the course of his speeches, hence my rendering.
6 *Can't you see:* lit., "know then that."
14 *the servants of my own house:* Taken from the beginning of verse 15.
17 *my presence:* This could well be translated "my breath," but I doubt such a trivial and undignified sense and it would certainly be laughable to an English audience.
   relatives: This could be translated "my children" (see Pope, *Job,* p. 132).
18 *jeer and taunt:* lit., "speak against me."
20 A difficult verse to translate and probably is out of context, so I have deleted it.
24 *Engraved by iron stylus on lead:* (see Pope, *Job,* p. 134.)
26 *decayed away:* The Hebrew expression is difficult and the text may be corrupt, but no one has come up with a compelling emendation or alternative interpretation.
26 *without my flesh:* The Hebrew could mean "from my flesh," i.e., while Job is still in the flesh, though dead, or "without my flesh," i.e., as a disembodied soul.
27 *I feel relaxed inside:* Job experiences something in his chest or stomach, but it is not entirely clear what. I have taken the sentence as speaking of a positive feeling, rather than the negative or ambiguous one usually found here.

20:2 *reverberate:* lit., "answer me."
3 *a spirit within me:* lit., "a spirit out of my understanding (or intellect)."
7 *follow his own dung:* lit., "he perishes forever like his dung."
9 *He is mere appearance without substance, without a permanent place in the whole:* lit., "The eye that looked on him will not do so again, it will not again espy him in his place." My radically deviant rendering is an attempt to articulate the philosophical doctrine suggested by these rather pale statements of the friends.
13 *in his teeth:* lit., "on his palate."
16 *bitter juice:* lit., "snake/spider poison."
17 *taste:* lit., "see."
   of oil: Emending the text to yield this sense.
18 *nor consume the return from his toil:* Emending slightly to yield this sense.

19 *toil:* Emending the vowels to yield this sense.
22 *When he reaches,* etc.: Translating loosely for smoother poetry.
23 *feed him flame for bread:* Hebrew uncertain, translated to continue the poetic image.
25 Deleted because it is too corrupt to make good sense.
28 *pilfered:* Emending slightly to yield this sense.

21:6 *backbone:* lit., "flesh."
7 *an evil man:* Most of verses 7-16, 17-33 are plural—evil men, they, etc., but I found it easier and more vivid to use the singular.
8 *he watches them strike root:* Supplied for a stronger statement, the Hebrew reading: "their issues with their (own) eyes."
11 *to play:* Supplied to match the second line of the couplet.
skip and dance: Translating one Hebrew word twice.
12 *He and his family:* The Hebrew simply has "they."
play: lit., "lift up," perhaps with an implied "voice," *viz.,* sing.
13 *dies peacefully in his sleep:* lit., "they go (to) Sheol quickly," probably meaning an "easy death," hence my rendering.
14 *We don't want anything to do with You:* lit., "We take no pleasure in the knowledge of Your ways."
15 *Now, isn't he master:* Emended to yield this sense. The second line of the verse doesn't fit Job and may indicate that the first line should not be emended, but the whole verse be attributed to a pious commentator.

24:1-4, 9, 12, 22-23, 25 Chapter 24 is a crazy patchwork of utterances requiring our pick-and-choose procedure. The verses selected here continue Job's refutation of his friends' dogma of punishments for the wicked. They do not belong after the rupture of relationship, so they must be associated with chapter 21 (the only other place Job challenges his friends' dogma). They fit chapter 21 nicely by providing a description of what the sinners, whose fate deviates so from the dogma about them, actually do to others.
2 *The scoundrel:* Emended to supply a subject; again translating a Hebrew plural as a singular.
robs pasturage: lit., "and they pasture (them)."
3 *confiscates:* lit., "drive away" or "carry away."
forecloses: lit., "takes in pledge," an act not particularly immoral.
5-8 These verses describe the wretched existence of people being hounded from the civilized world, reminding one of chapter 30:1-10. Deleted as unfitting here.
9 *infant:* Emending a vowel to yield this sense.
10-11. These verses continue the description of verses 5-8. Deleted.
12 *dying:* Emending a vowel to yield this sense.
13-17 Deleted as out of context, describing the "rebel against the light."
18-21, 24 Deleted as inappropriate to Job. They describe the terrible fate of the wicked.

23 *and support:* lit., "he (the human who is benefited) is supported."

21:17 *oppressor:* Continuing to put the Hebrew plural in the singular (see comments for 21:7, 24:2).
scheming boomerang: lit., "their misfortune come upon them."
distribute suffering equitably: lit., "He distributes suffering in His wrath."
18 *How often:* Supplied from previous verse.
20 *his downfall:* The Hebrew word is uncertain.
God's: lit., "Almighty's." We have not been translating the names of God with rigid consistency, for often the Hebrew usage sounds naïve in English.
22 Deleted as out of context, a comment by an offended commentator.
24 *blessed in prosperity,* etc.: A loose rendering of the Hebrew summarizing its meaning while abandoning the contrived imagery.
28 *survived:* Supplied from context.
29 *merchants and pilgrims who pass through our region on the highway:* Naming the types of "travelers" (in Hebrew).
33 *Before and after his casket,* etc.: I have reversed the order of lines and made the image of a funeral procession more explicit.
34 *hold any weight,* lit., "There is nothing left (of your arguments) but falsehood."

22:2 *a man's intelligence:* lit., "a prudent or intelligent (man)."
for his own good: lit., "to him," either to God or to himself.
3 *Has the Almighty shown delight:* lit., "Is there delight to the Almighty."
6 *foreclosed on loans:* lit., "take pledge."
8 *You've:* Supplied to make a complete sentence.
10 *walk in a maze:* lit., "surround you."
11 *Your eyes cannot penetrate the fallen darkness:* lit., "or (in) darkness you cannot see."
12 *Look above:* Supplying "above" to suggest that the sentence invites Job to consider how high God is by contemplating the height of the stars.
13 *of earthly affairs:* Supplied to give the sentence an object.
15 *all:* Added for emphasis.
18 Deleting the second line of the verse as an editorial comment.
20 *Aren't our enemies:* The verb and subject do not agree in Hebrew.
all that would remain: lit., "what they left."
21 *your fortunes will be reversed:* lit., "goodwill come to you."
22 *my friend:* Supplied to personalize the address.
as a rule of life: lit., "in your heart."
23 *humble yourself:* Emended to yield this sense.
24-25 Deleted as inappropriate in this context.
26 *Stand erect:* lit., "lift your face."
29 *those who exalt themselves:* Emended to yield this sense.
30 *the innocent:* Emending or interpreting in this sense.

27:5-6 These verses have been moved here as a very suitable introduction to Job's last speech (23:2 is totally out of place for such a dramatic moment). Job rejects the charges made by Eliphaz and turns his back on his companions.

27:5 *God forbid:* This is simply an adverb of denial in the Hebrew, it does not contain "God."
  6 *hold it fast in this fist and never relax my grip:* lit., "I will not relinquish (it)."
    my conscience: lit., "my heart."
    for one day of my life: lit., "my days."

23:5 *His reasoning:* lit., "what He says to me."
  8-9 These verses interrupt the train of thought, though they do suit Job's desperate search for God.
  10 *the way of my going:* lit., "the way with me."
    If: Supplied by context.
  12 *committed to heart:* Emended to yield this sense.
  13 *if He has arrived at His decision:* Emended from "in one" or "in himself" to "He chooses."
    He is free to do his arbitrary whim: lit., "His soul desires and He does."
  14 *my decreed destiny:* lit., "my decree."
    more tortures in mind: lit., "many like them (= more of the same) are with Him."
  15 *The very thought of Him strings me up:* lit., "I think and I tremble at Him."
  16 *weak-willed:* lit., "timid."
  17 *Am I not:* There is nothing in the Hebrew suggesting that this is a question, but the only other expedient would be to delete the "not."
    enveloped in: lit., "destroyed before," but that meaning is too strong for this situation.
    my way concealed from me in gloom: lit., "gloom conceals from my face."

27:11-12, 28:1-27 The Hebrew text as it stands attributes chapters 27 and 28 to Job. The verses from chapter 27 are variously attributed to Job and Zophar by scholars, and chapter 28 is regularly removed from the mouth of all the speakers as an intrusion. 27:11-12 seem to me to make an acceptable introduction to chapter 28. Together they make a nice interlude between the dialogue portion of the book and Job's final large speech and God's answer. I have given the speech to the narrator.
27:11 *what He has at His disposal:* lit., "what is with the Almighty."
  12 *already know:* lit., "have perceived."
    live with such cheap thoughts: lit., "are you vain (with) vanity."

112

28:1 *is found:* Emended to yield this sense.
  3 *Men sink shafts, etc.:* A loose translation.
  4 *far below the surface:* lit., "from with dwelling," meaning probably "away from (i.e., below) where humans dwell."
  5 *harvest:* lit., "bread."
  9 *Man alone:* Supplied to designate the subject precisely.
11 *probes the very sources of rivers:* See Pope, *Job,* pp. 175, 180-181.
18 *any precious thing:* The Hebrew names a specific stone, but the identity is uncertain, so I used the opportunity to generalize.
19 *on the same scale:* lit., "Ethiopian topaz cannot equal it . . . it cannot be weighed on scales (bought) with pure gold."
22 *underworld:* lit., "Abaddon and death."
26 *gave . . . their vocation:* lit., "way."
27 *scrutinized it minutely:* lit., "and also scrutinized it."
28 Deleted as out of tone with the exalted reflection of chapter 28.

29:5 *when my way:* lit., "with me."
  6 *in wine:* The Hebrew word means "curds" or "cheese," a rather far-fetched image, and even "milk" would hardly conjure up satisfying associations. Treading out grape juice would.
29:21-25 These verses continue the description of Job's position in his community in time past, and so I have moved them here.
23 *tongue out:* lit., "mouth open."
24 *resist:* lit., "throw down, make fall."
18 *in old age:* Emended to yield this sense: See Pope, *Job,* 189.
19 *refreshed:* lit., "lodges in my branches."
20 *My potency will grow with effort:* The probable meaning of the Hebrew: "My bow will flourish in my hand."

30:1 *young hoodlums:* lit., "meaner than I for days," meaning younger but also contemptible and belonging to a contemptible class or race (as one can see from the following verses).
  3 *They are:* Supplying a subject and finite verb.
   grubbing about the desolate, deserted steppe: The Hebrew is uncertain.

  5 *settled areas:* lit., "middle, interior," perhaps civilized areas.
   chased: lit., "shouted."
  6 *forced:* Supplied.
   Hollowed out: Supplied.
  7 *wild squeals and grunts:* Translating the same Hebrew word twice.
   there: The Hebrew has "under nettles."
10 *They treat me as an untouchable:* lit., "They despise me, they keep far from me."
11 *undo my belt:* Emended to yield this sense.
12 *a mob:* Hebrew word uncertain.
   chases me along a road: lit., either "they send my feet" or "my feet send." The exact meaning is unclear, but a chase would seem a plausible interpretation.

blocks my way of escape: lit., "they heap up ways of oppression/misery against me."

30:13 *cuts off the footpath I pursue:* lit., "tear up my path."
  15 *is pursued:* Emending the vowels to yield this sense.
  16 *I have been drained of life:* lit., "my soul is poured out from me," actually "upon me." My translation follows the interpretation of Pope, *Job,* p. 195.
  18 *jerks:* Emended to yield this sense.
     grabs: Emended to yield this sense.
  22 *wild storm:* Emended to yield this sense.
  23 *appointment:* lit., "house of meeting."
  24 *sinking man:* Emended to yield this sense.
     cry for help: Emended to yield this sense.
  27 *get the jump:* lit., "go before me" or "meet me."

27:2-4 Chapter 31 needs an introduction to its series of disclaimers and chapter 27 has just the words needed, an oath promising that the disclaimers are true.
  3 *in my chest:* lit., "in me."
     breath of life: lit., "breath of God."

31:6 This verse challenging God to examine his life fits well after the oath, while it breaks the natural connection between verses 5 and 7.
     God: Introducing the subject in the first line rather than the second.
     scales of justice: lit., "scales of right" or "right scales."
  1 *imposed a ban:* follow Pope's translation of "cut a covenant" here, *Job,* pp. 197, 200.
     never: Again following Pope, p. 200.
  2 *If I succumbed:* Supplied to make the idea more explicit.
     my reward . . . my inheritance: The personal references are lacking in the Hebrew.
     the exalted Lord: lit., "the Almighty from on high."
  3 *destined for . . . in store for:* The Hebrew simply has "for" in both cases.
     nihilists: lit., "workers of wickedness," with the word translated "wickedness" also suggesting nothingness, falsehood.
  4 *God:* Supplied for the Hebrew "He."
  7 *but a step:* lit., "my step strayed from the path."
     or stained my hands: lit., "a stain stuck to my hand."
  8 *planting:* The Hebrew word could mean a range of things, from "what I produce by my labor" to "my offspring."

38-40 These three verses about Job's treatment of his cropland in anticlimactic at the end of the chapter, so most commentators move it here.

114

38 *sought restitution:* lit., "wept together."
39 *powers of the soil:* lit., the "lords" or even "Baals" of the land.
10 *cuckold me:* lit., "bend down upon her."
11 *committed adultery:* lit., "it is lewdness."
   a serious breach of morality: lit., "offense (punishable) by judges."
12 *even beyond death:* lit., "a fire devouring unto Abaddon."
13 *suit against me:* The Hebrew says "their suit," and an emendation
   to "her" is necessary to yield the sense I have given it.
15 *my Creator:* lit., "the One who made me in the womb made him."
   who fashioned us: lit., "He fashioned us in the womb, one."
18 *All my life,* etc.: A loose rendering.
21 *accused one:* lit., "waved my hand," the context indicating that
   this would harm the disadvantaged.
   among the judges: Supplied to explain the reference.
23 *feared God's judgment:* lit., "the calamity of God is fearful to me."
25 *in being a self-made man:* lit., "that my hand has acquired
   much."
27 *a gesture of worship:* lit., "my hand kissed my mouth."
28 *serious sins:* lit., "iniquity of my judges."
   transcendent God: lit., "God on high."
30 *in prayer:* lit., "in oath" or "curse."
31 *who is not filled with meat:* The question might be understood in a
   sexual sense: see Pope, *Job,* pp. 207-8, but I have followed the con-
   ventional interpretation.
33 *from men:* lit., "like a man" or "like Adam."
   in my memory: lit., "in my bosom."
34 *may I become:* The Hebrew reads: "for I feared . . ." or perhaps "if
   I feared . . . " but we need a punishment at this point.
   ostracism: lit., "scorn."
   my clan: The Hebrew lacks the personal reference.
35 *He had heard:* lit., "O that for me there was one to listen to me."
   The reference is obviously to God.
   my X: In Hebrew, "my tau," which was written like an "x."
   indictment: lit., "a document."
36 *be proud:* Supplied to stress the positive nature of the action.
37 I have reversed the sequence of lines.
   stride before Him: lit., "draw near Him."
   as a noble before his king: The Hebrew has only "like a noble," but
   I have made the image more explicit.

Chapters 32-37 Deleted as an intrusion composed by a reader
   offended by the outcome of the dialogue.

38:1 *The Lord:* Using the traditional substitute for the sacrosanct and
   unutterable divine name, YHWH (vocalized by scholars as
   "Yahweh").
  2 *muddles the discussion:* lit., "darken counsel," open to several interpretations. The word "counsel" can mean both the process of

deciding and what has been decided. I have taken the first option.

3   *Take your stand:* In the Hebrew, God challenges Job to prepare for battle. Since the Lord is actually going to examine Job, I have changed the line slightly to evoke a court scene as much as a military one.
I will interrogate you: lit., "I will ask you." I want to underline the court setting.
and you will testify: lit., "you will cause me to know." Again I have selected a word evoking the court setting.

5   *Who drew up, etc.:* The Hebrew interjects at the end of this line "that you know," which could be translated with the taunt "surely you know," but it is too distracting.

7   *heavenly beings:* lit., "sons of God."

8   *Were you there:* The Hebrew lacks this phrase, but something of this sort is needed.
from its source: lit., "from the womb," a highly metaphorical or mythological way of speaking of the origin of the sea.

9   *covered it:* lit., "(made) darkness its swaddling clothes," continuing the birth metaphor.
deep blue: lit., "darkness," or "dark clouds."

10 *decreed its extent:* lit., "clamped my ordinance upon it."

12 *given the dawn its orders:* lit., "have you caused the dawn to know its place," perhaps a mythological idea of dawn as a divine being who is "posted," as Pope, *Job,* p. 251, suggests.

13 *its occupants:* lit., "wicked." Specifying the earth's inhabitants as "wicked" doesn't add anything suitable to the statement.

14 *dyed dapply:* Emended to yield this sense.

15 *just as quickly:* Added to give a sense of time.
robbed of light: The Hebrew reads: "Their light is withdrawn from the wicked." Again designating the inhabitants as wicked does not add anything, unless the whole verse is a moralistic comment about the punishment of the wicked.
while people are still at work: lit., "The poised arm is shattered." This could be a reference to the thwarting of the attack of the wicked, but I have taken it as a more neutral statement about the fall of night while people are still engaged in their daily tasks.

17 *archway to the dark land:* lit., "gates of the shadow of death."

18 *mapped:* lit., "comprehend."
detail the features: lit., "declare."

20 *Can you . . . :* Dependent clauses in Hebrew.
them . . . their . . . their: Singular in Hebrew, referring either to darkness or light of verse 19.

21 *You would know:* Conditional supplied.
your life had spanned the ages: lit., "number of your days were many."

23 *nature wages:* Added to provide a finite clause.

24 *distribution center for the wind:* lit., "where light is distributed from." Emending "light" to "wind."

25 *regulates the flow:* lit., "digs a ditch for."
directs the flight: lit., "a way for."
26 *channels . . . even:* Verb supplied from verse 25, distinguishing the act of causing a rainstorm from that of causing rain to fall on uninhabited regions.
deserts and peaks: Translating the same word twice.
29 *To which dam can you trace . . . :* lit., "who has given birth to the hoarfrost of heaven?"
30 *which:* Supplied to subordinate this pair of lines; the verbs have been changed from reflexive to active, with "hoarfrost" as the subject.
hardens: Emended to yield this sense.
32 *signs of the Zodiac:* The meaning of the Hebrew word is disputed and could well be the name of one heavenly sign.
Great Bear: The meaning of the Hebrew is uncertain.
33 *laws of heavenly bodies:* lit., "statutes of heaven."
their influence: lit., "its (heaven's?) rule (or message)."
34 *bring down a shower:* lit., "a shower of rain cover you."
35 *Does lightning obey your orders?:* lit., "Can you send forth (your orders) in the lightnings and they go?"
36 *in the elements:* The meaning of the Hebrew word is unknown, but the context demands a meteorological phenomenon.
the weather: The meaning of the Hebrew word is unknown.
taught . . . a pattern: lit., "give . . . understanding."
37 *water tanks:* lit., "jars" or "skins of heaven."

39:1 *inform:* Emending the vowels to read "cause to know" rather than simply "know," as it is now.
3 *their wombs open:* lit., "they let their young break forth."
5 *wild ass:* There are two words in verse 5 with this meaning, so I have substituted "it" in the second line.
halter and harness: lit., "bonds."
6 *Who adapts,* etc.: Translated as an independent question rather than a dependent clause with God as subject, as it is in Hebrew.
8 *the countryside:* Added for parallelism.
9-12: This challenge regarding the buffalo does not fit the context. It does not ask Job whether he can do only what God can do, as the genuine passages do.
13-18: This passage is not even a challenge, but a description of the odd behavior of the ostrich. It does not suit the interrogation of Job. Interestingly, some Septuagint manuscripts lack these verses, perhaps supporting our contention that they are not original.
19 *spirit:* The Hebrew word can mean either "strength" or "courage."
send quivers: The Hebrew words could mean "clothe with mane," as in Pope, pp. 262-263.
21 *lunges forward:* Translated somewhat loosely.
22 *disdain:* lit., "he laughs . . . and is not alarmed."
close combat: lit., "mouth of the sword."
23 *whizzing by:* The meaning of the Hebrew is uncertain.

30 This verse seems out of keeping with the description of hawks and eagles, which focuses on their capacity to soar to great heights and perch on inaccessible spots.

40:1 This verse repeats 38:1 and is unnecessary here, indeed awkward, since Job has not yet replied to the Lord. Hence we have left it out.

2 *continue to dispute:* Adding the words "continue to" to indicate that it is not a question of whether it can be done, but whether Job will persevere after God's address.
deity: lit., the "Almighty."
accuses: Or "reproves."
these questions: lit., "it."

4 *I plead silence:* lit., "I put my hand on my mouth."

7 See 38:3.

8 *prove your innocence:* lit., "that you may be justified."

9 *like a god . . . like one:* lit., "like God . . . like His."

12 *despots:* lit., "wicked."
beneath your feet: lit., "beneath them."

14 *for you will have proven that you have the power to save yourself:* lit., "for your right hand will save you."

15-24 These verses describing Behemoth do not fit the context. The passage does not challenge Job to be God, as the genuine passages do. It is simply the description of an unusual beast, probably a hippopotamus. The following passage on Leviathan, on the other hand, does suit the context.

41:1 *from the ocean depths:* Added to explain to the reader where this monster was thought to live.

3 *pour out . . . supplications . . . motivate you . . . with flattery:* These phrases describe human prayer directed to God. In other words, Job is asked whether he can assume the position of God.

5 *like a peacock:* Added for color and concreteness.

6 This verse shifts to third person plural and from an interrogative to an indicative sentence. These shifts make it unsuitable to the passage.

7 *plant:* lit., "fill," but the idea is not of planting many harpoons rather than few, but of planting any at all.

9 *hope of conquest:* lit., "hope."
defeated gods: Emended to yield this sense.

11 *Who . . . ?:* Emended to yield this sense.

41:12-34 These verses continue to treat Leviathan, but they no longer challenge Job to act like God. They resemble 40:15-24 in describing an unusual beast, this time a crocodile.

42:2 *Now:* Added to underline the new recognition expressed in these lines.

3a The Hebrew begins this verse with words appropriate to God ("Who is this who muddles the discussion without knowledge?"), repeating 38:2 almost verbatim. It must be here by mistake.

3bc The Hebrew of these two lines lends itself to several, rather contradictory translations. The usual interpretation of the verse is
that Job repudiates what he said earlier ("I spoke of things I did
not know . . . "), but I take it as a positive declaration of praise of
God for his incomprehensible wonders. I have translated the verb
as a present tense and the object ("wonders") as God's saving
deeds, and the two statements forswearing claims to understanding as interjections expressing amazement.

4 This verse consists of words appropriate to God ("Listen, please,
and I will speak, I will interrogate you and you will testify").
Again, we must have a misplaced variant of 38:3 and 40:7.

5 See my discussion of this verse in the chapter entitled "How This
Book Came to Be."

6 This may be the most controversial translation to be offered in
this book. The common translation is *repent in* dust and ashes."
The other passages in the Bible using the Hebrew word translated
"repent" with the preposition translated "in" (or "upon") do not
support this traditional rendering, but rather something like "repent of" or "forswear." My interpretation is that Job does not re-
cant and show remorse for what he had said earlier, but rather
declares his abandonment of mourning for joy and praise. I have
argued this case in greater detail *Vetus Testamentum,* Vol. XXVI,
pp. 369-371.

8 *truthfully:* This translates a Hebrew noun meaning "truth, cor-
rect," covering both objective truth and personal truthfulness.
entreaty: lit., "I will accept him," even more lit., "I will lift up his
face."
foolishly: The Hebrew noun is elsewhere used only of human actions of an obscene and immoral character (rape, adultery). It is
rather strange to hear God speak of his righteous judgment as acting foolishly (irrationally out of anger?), but that is indeed what
He says unless the text should be emended.

11 *the many misfortunes:* lit., "all the evil."

14 The meaning of the three daughters' names: (1) Dove, (2) Cin-
namon, (3) Horn of Kohl; see Pope, p. 292.

17 *fulfilled:* lit., "full of days."

Bibliography

The work that has most influenced my interpretation of Job:

Claus Westermann, *Der Aufbau des Buches Hiob.* Beiträge zur historischen Theologie 23. J. C. B. Mohr (Paul Siebeck) Tubingen, 1956.

The best commentaries in English on the Hebrew text and its translation:

Edouard-Paul Dhorme, *A Commentary on the Book of Job.* Trans. Harold Knight. Nelson, 1967.

Marvin H. Pope, *Job. The Anchor Bible,* Vol. 15. Doubleday & Co., Inc., 1965.

Good commentaries in English on the meaning of the Book of Job:
Samuel Terrien, *The Book of Job. Introduction and Exegesis.* The Interpreter's Bible, Vol. 3. Abingdon Press, 1954.
Samuel Terrien, *Job, Poet of Existence.* Bobbs-Merrill Co., Inc., 1957.

A popular essay on Job by an evangelical author:
H. Harold Kent, *Job, Our Contemporary.* Eerdmans Publishers, 1967.

A profound retelling of Job's story by a modern Jewish novelist is found in:
Elie Wiesel, *Messengers of God: Biblical Portraits and Legends.* Random House, 1976.

An excellent survey of the interpretations of Job, past and present:
Nahum N. Glatzer, *The Dimensions of Job: A Study and Selected Readings.* Schocken, 1969.

Two scholarly articles that I have written on aspects of Job:
"The Translation of Job XLII 6," Short Note, *Vetus Testamentum* XXVI (1976), pp. 369-71.
"Job's Address of God," to be published in the future.